# RIDING THE WAVE

*Leading the Local Church
from Message to Mission*

DR. T.D. STUBBLEFIELD

Riding the Wave – Leading the Local Church from Message to Mission

Copyright © 2020 T. D. Stubblefield Ministries, L.L.C.

ISBN 978-0-578-64170-6

Library of Congress Control Number 2020901773

All rights reserved. No portion of this book may be reproduced, stored in a retrieval system, or transmitted in any form or by any means— electronic, mechanical, photocopy, recording, scanning, or other— except for brief quotations in critical reviews or articles, without the prior written permission of the publisher.

All Scripture quotations, unless otherwise indicated, are taken from the Holy Bible, King James Version.

Scripture quotations marked NIV are taken from the Holy Bible, New International Version. © 1973, 1978, 1984, 2011.

Scripture quotations marked MSG are taken from The Message by Eugene Peterson. © 1993, 1994, 1995, 1996, 2000, 2001, 2002.

Scripture quotations marked TLB are taken from The Living Bible. © 1971.

Scripture quotations are taken from the Moffatt Translation. © 1922, 1924, 1926, 1935.

Cover Design by Younge Clark Creative

Cover Photo Taken by Dr. T. D. Stubblefield in April 2019
While On Sabbatical in Carolina Beach, North Carolina

Printed in the United States by
Graphic Connections Publishing, Chesterfield, Missouri 63005

# TRIBUTES

**Ronald Clifton**
**FBCC - 2000 - Present**

My first interaction with Pastor T. D. Stubblefield (Pastor) was in late 1999. He came to the First Baptist Church of Chesterfield (FBCC) to preach a sermon during the church's search for a new Pastor. After hearing him preach, my wife and I were so impressed, that we decided that if he were chosen to be the Pastor of the church, we would join on the very first Sunday that he preached. The Pastor was selected by the church and our family joined on that very first Sunday in February 2000.

That first Sunday in February 2000 has led to a spiritual bond between Pastor and I that has endured and never wavered through some of life's most difficult challenges. Pastor is not only an excellent preacher of the Word of God, but also a superior teacher as well. I am both proud and honored to call T. D. Stubblefield not only my Pastor, but also my friend and brother in Christ.

Ronald Clifton

**Terrence Hardin**
**FBCC 2006 - 2015**

During the time my company relocated me and my family from Baton Rouge, Louisiana to St. Louis, Missouri, I served as an active member at the First Baptist Church of Chesterfield under the leadership of Dr. T. D. Stubblefield. His relationship with my family begin in an unofficial "watch care" type of scenario in which we faced a family crisis only 2 weeks after having moved into our home in O'Fallon, Missouri. My daughter was diagnosed with end stage renal disease at the age of 10.

Devastated by this sudden news, I knew I needed a local church family in our corner. We had attended the church 3 consecutive Sundays, but made it a point to introduce ourselves to Pastor and his lovely wife Judy after each service because his presentation of God's Word was so effective as a tool for daily living. I only called the church for prayer and petitioned the receptionist who took the call to tell the Pastor, "... it's the family who moved here from Louisiana..." That Sunday, while in the Cardinal Glennon Children's Hospital, I heard the sound of cowboy boots coming down the hallway and stopped in our room. Standing in the doorway, was Pastor Stubblefield saying, "You need a church family beside you right now. Whether you unite with us or not, we have already adopted this family".

And for the entire time we lived in Missouri until I transferred to Atlanta, Georgia in 2015, that is the relationship this Pastor-Teacher had with my family - personal, caring and giving - even with all the responsibilities on a full time pastor with a congregation of that size. His love for reading and learning serves as the foundation for his skill set that makes him an effective Pastor-Teacher with the wisdom of Paul and the heart of David. He still is "My Pastor". Thanks for being a faithful follower of God's Holy Spirit in the care of His Church and in the building of His Kingdom. Continue to make men Disciples of Christ!

Terrence Hardin

**Henry James**
**FBCG - 1988 - 2009**
**FBCC - 2010 - Present**

Congratulations on the occasion of your fourth book, Dr. T.D. Stubblefield. One of the greatest blessings of my life has been my relationship with you as my Pastor-Teacher, and friend. Shortly after our first meeting in 1988, you became my pastor and mentor while leading our congregation in Georgetown, KY where your preaching, teaching, and nurturing resulted in not only church growth, but more importantly, in spiritual growth among the members and within the community. Providentially, after nearly a decade apart while working in different areas of the country, I found myself under your pastoral care once again when I joined our church in Chesterfield, MO.

During the past 32 years as I have journeyed from a career in business and industry to my current role as faculty and mentor in higher education, I have observed closely your leadership and effectiveness. You have been a great pastoral leader with much wisdom to share to benefit others, particularly emerging Christian leaders. You love God's word and God's people. You live God's word – let the people see the word you teach and preach not just hear it. You do this by living a dedicated, purposeful, exemplary yet imperfect life. It is an honor and a privilege to call you my pastor and friend and to acknowledge your long history of effective pastoral leadership and caregiving for God's people.

Henry T. James, MBA, ABD

**Dr. DaMaris Jones**
**FBCC - 2015 - Present**

I have been blessed to be under the covering of Dr. T.D. Stubblefield for the past 5 years at First Baptist Church of Chesterfield. Pastor T.D. Stubblefield has exemplified the essence of true servant leadership through his commitment to God, denial of self, humility, integrity, modeling and love for God's people. My spiritual journey has been enriched and strengthened because of the intentional charge of Pastor Stubblefield to teach and preach the Gospel without compromising and conforming to the opinions and lifestyles of the world. Pastor Stubblefield is renowned in his own right who leads by example.

DaMaris A. Jones, Ed.D.
Principal, St. Louis Public Schools

**Sandra Young**
FBCG - 1989 - 1999

There's so much I could write about my experiences at First Baptist Church Georgetown under your leadership. I'll never forget the time we had a fire at our home in New Zion and First Baptist sent us a love offering. When Dale was out of work you were so encouraging and always asked about how he was doing and that he would find employment soon. And we weren't members of First Baptist at the time. I had been attending Training for Service, Sunday School and Sunday morning worship for several months. But it was that one Sunday during the invitation following Sunday School that you said, "You should worship where you serve and serve where you worship." That's when I made the decision to join the fellowship and faith family at First Baptist Church Georgetown. And the rest is history. I'm ever so grateful to God for the love and friendship from you, Sis. Judy, and your family. I pray God's continued blessings for your family and ministry.

Your friend & sister-in-Christ,
Sandi

# ACKNOWLEDGEMENTS

I have been privileged by God's grace and mercy to serve as pastor-teacher of two congregations with rich and storied histories - both founded by slaves before the beginning of the Civil War—the First Baptist Church of Georgetown, Kentucky in 1842 and the First Baptist Church of Chesterfield, Missouri in 1846. These congregations have provided the succulent soil that absorbed the sacred seeds God providentially placed in the heart, mind and spirit of this pastoral sower. Coupled with the water of His Word and the heat and help of His Spirit, our shared, and at times, straitened experiences of ministry became the opulent gardens where many of the paradigms, principles, and perspectives shared in these pages find their genesis. These faith families provided the spiritual, relational and vocational space where I have strived for almost four decades now to open the minds, hold the hands and touch the hearts of those God placed in my spiritual care. Together, we have strived to synchronize truth, tradition, and transition in our mutual endeavor to be the church and change the world.

An innumerable company of witnesses, workers and worshippers have strengthened my heart, head and hands for this present work with their constructive cooperation, wise counsel, fervent prayers and constant encouragement. This bountiful and blessed band of spiritual brothers and sisters has contributed to the shaping of the preaching, pastoral and leadership perspectives categorized and catalogued in the following pages. Like the Apostle Paul, "I am a debtor" to so many.

I am particularly grateful to Dr. David Larsen, Professor Emeritus of Preaching at Trinity Evangelical Divinity School in Deerfield, Illinois who, over ten years ago as the mentor for my doctoral project, encouraged enthusiastically the sharing of the accretions of that research with a larger audience. *Riding the Wave* is my acceptance of that distant yet timely summons.

I am also thankful for the proficient, perceptive and professional proofing and editing of the original manuscript of this book by Deidra Scott-Elbert. Her corroboration on yet another literary project gives me great joy.

And I dare not neglect to mention the stellar support, wise counsel and organizational savvy of Dr. Kimberly Hodge-Bell, Administrative Assistant for T. D. Stubblefield Ministries. She encourages my pursuit of excellence with both a tough mind and a tender heart.

Our Assistant Pastor, Reverend Christopher Rogers, has calibrated and celebrated with me so much that is recorded in these pages. As a spiritual father to his son, I am grateful to God for giving me the vantage and the view to observe his growth and maturation as a man, minister, preacher, pastor, husband and father. We have both been sharpened and shaped by a special relationship that is characterized by trust, truth and transparency. And as my pastoral journey at First Baptist Church of Chesterfield nears completion, I applaud Traci Wright, our Office Assistant for her "motherly management' of my busy schedule, ministry commitments, archiving and valuable administrative support. Her stewardship and steadiness is a blessing to our Faith Family.

Finally and fervently, I must offer sincere adulation and appreciation to my wife Judy, my soul mate and journey partner of forty-three years, Mother, Matriarch and Model to our four children and ten grandchildren whose unshakeable affection, untiring allegiance and unrelenting affirmation encourages me even in this season of ministry to pursue my passion. She will always be my pearl of great price.

To these and so many others whom the Lord has allowed to touch my life and me theirs, I say thank you for the journey and the joy.

# TABLE OF CONTENTS

**PART 1**     1
Riding the Wave: The Pastor as Preacher

    **Chapter 1**
    Introduction     3

    **Chapter 2**
    Preaching and the Biblical and Theological Foundations
    of the Church's Mission     9

    **Chapter 3**
    The Revelatory Constellation of Pastoral Preaching     17

    **Chapter 4**
    Preaching and Mission Holism - Part 1     25

    **Chapter 5**
    Preaching and Mission Holism Part 2     29

    **Chapter 6**
    The Pastor as Change Agent     43

**PART 2**     49
Riding the Wave The Pastor as Servant-Leader

    **Chapter 7**
    The Greatest Among You     51

    **Chapter 8**
    Diagnosing and Engaging the Congregational Culture     55

**Chapter 9**
Building Caring Community 63

**Chapter 10**
Leading and Leveraging Constructive Cooperation 73

**Chapter 11**
Creating Functional Structures 77

**Chapter 12**
Practicing Self Care 83

**Endnotes** 91

**Addendum** 97

PART 1

# RIDING THE WAVE:
## THE PASTOR AS PREACHER

CHAPTER 1

# INTRODUCTION

Recently, I spent a ministry sabbatical at beautiful Carolina Beach, North Carolina. I observed early one morning from my deck a number of surfers in the water. Adorned without exception in dark wet suits and with surfing boards in tow, some swam and others paddled from the shore out into the turbulent ocean while being submerged or rocked by the sporadic cascades of water from incoming waves. They shared a common purpose. Each waited until the right wave began its ascent and then quickly mounted it with their board for the swift and tumultuous ride toward the shore. This each did again and again with a childlike playfulness and adventuresomeness as the rhythmic roar of the vast ocean solicitously summoned them back into its bosom.

*Riding the Wave – Leading the Local Church from Message to Mission* is not a book about surfing but the metaphor is compelling. At a preaching conference a few years ago, I heard one presenter say that our primary task in pastoral ministry is to identify the wave that God is making and then mount and ride it. Being a part of what God is blessing is much more fulfilling and fruitful than asking God to bless what we are a part of! Just as God in infinite wisdom has created the vast oceans, when Jesus ascended back to glory, He gave gifts to the church. The Apostle Paul writes, ""And he gave some, apostles; and some, prophets; and some, evangelists; and some, pastors and teachers; for the perfecting of the saints, for the work of the ministry, for the edifying of the body of Christ" (Eph. 4:11-12 KJV). It is my sincere conviction that the gift and office of pastor-teacher is an oceanic wave that God uses to build the church and to advance the Kingdom of God. Needless to say, this recognition and reality is deeply humbling. Those who are called to serve the church in this office are submissive and sacred surfers who *ride the wave* created by the discovery, development and deployment of this unique spiritual gift. This occurs as the momentous message that is the Word of God is faithfully preached and taught "equipping the saints for the work of the ministry." The message and the mission, the Word and the work and the principles and practices of ministry are intertwined and interdependent.

In this opening salutation to you, admittedly I am aware as well that the phrase, "riding the wave" has another meaning or connotation in the popular culture. One dictionary says, "It is to enjoy the advantage or benefit of a particularly successful, popular, fortunate, interesting, etc., moment or period of time". This slant of meaning serves our purpose as well for who can dispute that the church our Lord and Savior Jesus Christ is building is ever pregnant with potential and promise because of His once for all sacrifice that is the redemptive capital that underwrites and assures our venture, victory and vindication as the people of God? Pastors, church leaders and every member of every local congregation are effectively riding the wave the Lord started over two-thousand years ago on a hill called Calvary!

Therefore, the mission of the local church to the world is an essential consequence of the proclamation of the Christian Gospel. The redeeming message of the cross compels the Christian evangel to the world. "For the preaching of the cross is to them that perish foolishness; but unto us which are saved it is the power of God" (1 Cor. 1:18 KJV). This dynamic is rooted in the risen Lord's Great Commission to the church recorded in Matt. 28:18-20. The casting, communicating and clarifying of the church's vision and mission are a primary focus and function of pastoral preaching in the local church.[1] Good preaching discourages our egotism, self-adulation and self-serving idolatries inspiring the sharing of the Gospel with those around us.[2]

The church is not a "one trick pony" but is multifaceted and multidimensional. This has certainly been the well substantiated case in my faith tradition - the African-American Baptist church. The church is not just a house of worship, but also a house of hope, culture, education, freedom and integrity. In the church, burdens are lifted, oneness experienced, self-esteem bolstered and hope rekindled. The Black preacher-pastor and preaching have always played a crucial role in this ongoing drama of renewal and transformation. The preacher is perceived and received by the people as called and set aside, and as one upon whom the Lord has laid His hands, the bountiful beneficiary of a special anointing from God. The preacher is expected to engage the Scriptures creatively, proclaiming redemption and restoration not only to the people but also <u>for</u> the people. The preacher's imagination takes rhetorical flight as dry bones come to life in desolate valleys, deliverance rides triumphantly on the wings of a dove and a rock becomes a hiding place.

Such preaching requires imagination and purpose and is pivotal and primary for communicating powerfully, profoundly and concretely to those in a particular social or situational praxis who are suffering disillusionment, oppression, disenfranchisement, hopelessness and lethargy. There are significant factors that make preaching and ministry in this social and cultural context unique and distinctive. First, historical reality and existing contingencies invite the constituents of oppressed classes who have embraced Christianity as creed and constitution to engage in urgent, critical reflection on the faith that bore and still bears us. Howard Thurman makes this point with excruciating clarity as he draws from the deep well and wealth of his own personal pilgrimage. It is incumbent upon those who speak to and for those traumatized by oppression in its variegated forms to engage in insightful interpretation and relevant exegesis of the Word of God as we speak words of comfort and consolation. This necessitates a distinctive polemic and apologetic in light of the dearth of substantive material for those with their backs against the wall.[3]

In the history of exegesis with its predominantly Euro-centric perspectives and interpretations, there is a partiality, albeit not always malicious, but nonetheless a bent toward the rich, the powerful and the advantaged in society. This often leaves those who must endure the legacy and reality of oppression with a Word that has been rendered sterile, muffled and conflicting. Needless to say, this is a hermeneutical challenge the Black preacher-pastor shares with clerics from other oppressed minorities as well. This disparity and deficiency is only compounded when the pedagogical structure of the university or seminary exclude cultural concerns and interpretive differences that African Americans bring to the exegetical and homiletical task. This is exactly the point William Myers makes in his analysis of the hermeneutical dilemma of the African American biblical scholar.[4]

In the second instance, powerful preaching in the African-American context is launched from a hermeneutic that affirms the ethic of Jesus Christ as the definitive elixir for what Thurman calls the "hounds of hell that dog the footsteps of the poor, the dispossessed and the disinherited".[5] This unholy trinity includes fear, deception and hatred. Preaching predicated on critical, creative and compelling exegesis of the text and the times (the experiential coordinates of the audience) aims both to illuminate and liberate.

When this type of preaching occurs, crippling and catastrophic fear is submerged in the ocean of a renewed self-esteem that is the birthright that Jesus gives to all that are oppressed. Deception is transformed into a simple yet profound authenticity that disarms the oppressor, empowers the oppressed and hobbles both pretense and advantage. Hatred is transfigured into a love so sincere and searching that those otherwise superficial boundaries are eradicated. Then the pulse of universality and the thread of commonality which make all human beings brothers and sisters are rediscovered and redefined. Of course the possibility of such universality presumes consistency to and concert with the Gospel of the Lord Jesus Christ, that old, old but eternally redeeming story of His death, burial and resurrection (1 Cor. 15: 1-4).

Finally, this particular and powerful legacy offers rich and plenteous spiritual ore for any faith tradition where pastoral preaching has as its ambitious aim to energize a mission perspective that propels the church toward a global and centrifugal mission to her immediate community, region and world. Serving as pastor and preacher in the African-American church tradition, my task has been informed by the need to affirm the rich spiritual, social and cultural heritage of two congregations whose birth and evolution are rooted in the crucible and cauldron of slavery.

In the final analysis, powerful, purposeful and passionate pastoral preaching aims to generate and accelerate activity while driving disciples from the church with the Gospel in head and heart.[6] Membership growth and ministry expansion ride on the spiritual wave created by the faithful execution of the pastor-teacher gift. Clear and compelling communication from the pulpit of the vision and mission of the local church is essential in order to encourage understanding, ownership and application by the congregation. As my mentor, the late Dr. Manuel Scott, Sr., once so aptly noted, "If there is a mist in the pulpit, there will be a fog in the pew."

*Riding the Wave – Leading the Local Church from Message to Mission* is a preaching and leadership model that can be used by pastors as a tool to mobilize their congregations around the vision and mission that God has placed in their hearts. The meager but I pray meaningful offerings in the following pages are colored, choreographed and contextualized by my own unique cultural and congregational experiences. My literary strivings here, like my preaching are admittedly autobiographical. But I pray the insights I share are relevant and relatable to any sincere and interested pastor's pursuit of excellence and effectiveness in ministry.

In Part 1, I will expose and explore the biblical and theological bedrock that undergirds the role of the pastor as a preacher. This portion of the book essentially offers up for consideration a theology of pastoral preaching. The words *preacher* and *pastor* are used interchangeably in this section with the recognition that while every pastor preaches, every preacher does not pastor.

In Part 2, the goal and objective is to share practical strategies that will enhance the pastor's role as a servant-leader. I am deeply humbled to do this in response to a plethora of appeals received over the years of ministry to codify in writing the intuitions, insights, initiatives, and interventions that have positively impacted the congregations God called me to serve and lead. This dual approach seeks to value and validate the effective integration and interface of these two roles - the pastor as preacher and the pastor as servant-leader as a magnificent and mounting wave that God uses to move the local church from message to mission.

CHAPTER 2

# PREACHING AND THE BIBLICAL AND THEOLOGICAL FOUNDATIONS OF THE CHURCH'S MISSION

A credible and coherent ministry vision worthy of communication through preaching to the congregation is not only rooted in the pastor's personal, spiritual and professional faith formation but also validated by sound biblical and theological underpinnings. A survey of relevant biblical and theological background that informed the development, execution and evaluation of this fundamental premise represent the merging of two critical and complementary streams of thought and reflection. First, what are some general descriptions, characteristics and concerns of pastoral preaching as it relates to the plausibility of preaching executed in the revelatory constellation that is the Word of God? Preaching is the extension of and expression of the supernatural revelation contained in scripture, which is communicated with particularity in the life of the local church by the pastor-teacher. Secondly, what is the relationship between preaching and the mission of God, the mission of the church and the unique calling of the pastor-teacher as preacher, missionary and change agent to the local congregation? Here, and in the succeeding chapters of Part 1, I will attempt to address these concerns.

## GENERAL DEFINITIONS, CHARACTERISTICS AND CONCERNS OF PASTORAL PREACHING

As previously noted, in a passage of primary reference, the Word of God describes the purpose of the spiritual gift of pastor-teacher. "It was he who gave some to be apostles, some to be prophets, some to be evangelists, and some to be pastors and teachers, to prepare God's people for works of service, so that the body of Christ may be built up" (Eph. 4:11-12 NIV). The word translated "perfecting" here is the Greek word *katartismon*. One meaning of this word is training and equipping soldiers for combat. The word is also used in the New Testament in a medicinal context that means setting back a bone that is broken (see 2 Cor. 3:11; 1 Thess. 3:10; 1 Pet. 5:10 and Mark 1:19).

The pastor-teacher equips the local church for the work of the ministry by exposing the truth of the scriptures while preaching and teaching. The ministry of the word creates spiritual cohesiveness and density in the church corporately and the life of the individual believer who is positive to the Word of God. Providing the supernatural sustenance that sustains the spiritual life of God's people is the chief task of the pastor.[1] Pastors lead and feed. Essentially, the feeding of the flock of God establishes and sustains the pastor's leadership and spiritual authority. This is the gift that God promised the backsliding nation of Judah in the Old Testament. "And I will give you pastors according to mine heart, which shall feed you with knowledge and understanding" (Jer. 3:15 KJV).

The faithful exercise of this gift will eventuate in a wave of synergy in the local church that has an outward focus. With ripple like reverberation, this wave begins in the innermost of spiritual consciousness and moves to the uttermost of ministry and missional engagement. Preaching exposes and discloses the facts about the human predicament and God's gracious offer of infinite power, privilege and possibility in God's universal Kingdom for everyone. Such status and significance is not the result of human effort and influence but rather assent by faith to the Gospel of the Lord Jesus Christ that allows us by grace to share the life of God (Eph. 2:8-10). Therefore, the pastor-teacher's task must necessarily and intentionally balance emphasis on both kerygma (proclamation of the Gospel) and didache (making disciples). Like the advancing movement of a train on two rails, both emphases are required or congregational ministry will be derailed and rendered sterile, shallow and superficial.

Sound biblical and expository preaching that compels others to an active and holy obedience in the priorities of the Kingdom is both art and craft. The pastor is a communicator of the Word of God. Altitude as well as aptitude characterizes the preaching of the pastor. Like Jacob's ladder, with its top in heaven and its base on earth, preaching is transacted on a pendulum that pulsates with inevitable tension. Preaching is a dialectic where divine treasure is wedded to human frailty. The Apostle Paul said, "But we have this treasure in earthen vessels, that the excellency of the power may be of God, and not of us" (2 Cor. 4:7 KJV). Preaching is the fusion of celestial and terrestrial horizons–-the biblical world recorded in Scripture and the experiential world of the believer.[2]

In the African-American faith tradition pastoral preaching is not a monologue but a dialogue. There is a distinctive dynamic of call and response that takes place between the preacher and the pew. But more is involved than a pulpit and an amen corner. In essence, preaching is trilateral communication. It engages both the vertical (theocentric) and horizontal (anthropocentric and egocentric) dimensions. Preaching involves the Ultra personal relationship with God, the intrapersonal relationship with self and interpersonal relationships with others.

For those who lie tragically crippled by the calamitous circumstances of life, the preacher's compassion and compelling communication engages and empowers their hobbling hurts at the gate that leads to and from authentic worship and powerful prayer (see Acts 3:1-11). With language that loves and lifts, the pastor-preacher assents and ascends to the same tone and tenor of the poet who said,

> "O Lord, how happy is the time
> When in Thy love I rest:
> When from my weariness I climb
> E'en to Thy tender breast.
> The night of sorrow endeth there,
> Thy rays outshine the sun;
> And in Thy pardon and Thy care
> The heaven of heavens is won (W. C. Dessler)

Exposition discloses the facts or ideas about something and provides viable and usable information about the intent, content and extent of the biblical text. Therefore, preaching involves the exposition of the preacher, the exposition of the text and the exposition of the audience. Literally the preacher is exposed within the living, intimate, transforming context of the preacher's relationship with the Lord Jesus Christ. Here, in the gymnasium of grace, the preacher participates in the exercise of godliness (1 Tim. 4:7).

Ultimately however, this private experience engages the Christian community. James M. Gordon says, "In a balanced spiritual life private discipline must be related to the experience of the Christian community, which provides a source of nurture, an informal corrective and link to the continuing Christian tradition".[3] This interface is possible and potent because the spirituality of the preacher permits openness, an inclusivity that reaches out and touches others. The transcendent and transforming Word that waters and refreshes the parched soul of the preacher, is part and parcel of the Word's dynamic descent into our lives. There it provides simultaneously "... seed to the sower, and bread to the eater" (Isa 55:10 KJV).

The faith community, the local church, is the point where the word of the Kingdom is launched. In every age of the church's demise, the prophetic vigilance of preaching has summoned the church back to her critical task of being a light to the world and the salt of the earth by reflecting the glory of Christ in worship, works and witnessing. Preaching is both declarative and <u>diagnostic,</u> and encourages the faith community to speak and act with unity and purposely concerning God's intent to a broken world.[4] While the preacher is called to preach the whole counsel of God, the tried truths of the Christian faith must be exposited and communicated to the congregation at a particular point and time. Preaching relates to life with all of its complexities and its myriad problems and possibilities but also compels us to reach beyond ourselves.[5] Preaching engages the experiential context of the people of God with a biblical message that equips the saints for the work of ministry and advances the Kingdom of God. The ministry of the Word is the heart of the pastoral task. The Apostle Paul reminded Timothy, "If thou put the brethren in remembrance of these things, thou shalt be a good minister of Jesus Christ, nourished up in the words of faith and of good doctrine, whereunto thou hast attained" (1 Tim. 4:6 KJV).

It was the marvelous genius of the slave preacher who, although untutored and unlearned, effectively wedded and weaved applicable elements of the biblical story into the slave's story producing a garment of praise and cementing the resolve among their destitute but determined supplicants to persevere amidst inexplicable suffering. The Negro <u>preacher</u> and the Negro <u>sorrow songs</u> or Black spirituals wailed and lamented this existential drama and difficulty with a depth that both transcended and transformed the experience of suffering.[6]

However, while Black preaching, singing and worship evolved in the particularized context and crucible of ignominious disenfranchisement, these insignias of our faith pilgrimage cannot remain there. The path to universal truth is by way of the particular. The incarnation of the Lord Jesus Christ is the quintessence of this reality and the consummate paradigm that informs the ministry of the local church. Miles Jones in an unpublished manuscript notes with great insight,

> Ethnic particularity is consistent with the promulgation of the Gospel. In Jesus Christ God has expressed in the intimacy of personal and inexhaustible uniqueness the divine desire for all people. Although it is a universal message designed for all, nevertheless, the specialness of a particular people and person are employed for use by God. Particular emphasis does not in any way destroy the significance of the Gospel. As a matter of fact, it makes it possible for those to whom it is directed particularly, to become instruments of the Eternal in a way that they might not be otherwise. Thus, ethnic particularity does not at all mean partiality.[7]

In the context of the pastor's passion and purpose to energize and actualize the congregation's commitment and response, one of the haunting, hobbling hazards of pastoral preaching is the inevitable frustration that ensues when it seems that preaching has fallen on deaf ears. It is during these times that Paul's admonition to Timothy resonates with urgency. "Preach the word; be instant in season, out of season; reprove, rebuke, exhort with all longsuffering and doctrine" (2 Tim. 4:2 KJV). Those "out of season" times can occur when preaching loses purposefulness and lacks substance and relevance to the maturation of disciples and the mission and ministry of the church. Dallas Willard says,

> Practical theology's overall task is, in effect, to develop for practical implementation the methods by which women and men interact with God to fulfill the divine intent for human existence. The intent for the church is twofold: the effective proclamation of the Christian gospel to all humanity, making "disciples" from every nation or ethnic group and the development of those disciples' character into the character of Christ himself.[8]

The "<u>what</u> shall we preach?" question is a matter of prayerful and purposeful intent and anticipates the question, how shall we preach?" The crucial issue then is how does preaching facilitate the process of moving people from faith to obedience and genuine Christ-likeness? This is especially challenging while preaching to cast, communicate, and clarify the mission and vision of the church that has evolved out of the preacher's own intimacy and interaction with God, the Word and the people or the flock of God. The preaching of Jesus, the greatest preacher of all, sought to draw those who had ears to hear and eyes to see into the effective orbit of God's will. Jesus reminded them and us as well that human potential is not the ultimate reference point but the Divine will for persons called out of darkness into His marvelous light. "But seek ye first the kingdom of God and his righteousness; and all these things shall be added unto you" (Matt. 6:33 KJV).

Undoubtedly, pastoral preaching presupposes the authority of the biblical tradition for the Bible speaks with timeless relevance to each new generation. Preaching is incarnational to the extent that it engages the experiential concerns of the believer. "For we preach not ourselves, but Christ Jesus the Lord; and ourselves your servants for Jesus' sake; For God, who commanded the light to shine out of darkness, hath shined in our hearts, to give the light of the knowledge of the glory of God in the face of Jesus Christ" (2 Cor. 4:5-6 KJV). The preacher-pastor is a "wounded healer" who trades both as merchant and consumer in the marketplace of life amidst the pain, paradox and possibilities of human existence moving always toward the relevant engagement of the problems of the day.

It is relevant because this type of preaching touches us at the point of our deepest needs and agony.[9]

CHAPTER 3

# THE REVELATORY CONSTELLATION OF PASTORAL PREACHING

Pastoral preaching presupposes the fundamental revelatory presupposition that the Church has historically proclaimed and posited as both normative and authoritative for salvation from sin, the crippling condition of human creatureliness. The particularity of this revelation as bound up in the life, death, resurrection and ascension of the Lord Jesus Christ, the Son of God is God's last word for <u>every</u> member of the human family and the <u>only</u> remedy for our existential estrangement. God has spoken definitively and decisively in and through Jesus Christ our Lord. This is powerful affirmation and prelude to the Book of Hebrews:

> God, who at sundry times and in divers manners spake in time past unto the fathers by the prophets, Hath in these last days spoken unto us by his Son, whom he hath appointed heir of all things, by whom also he made the worlds; Who being the brightness of his glory, and the express image of his person, and upholding all

things by the word of his power, when he had by himself purged our sins, sat down on the right hand of the Majesty on high. (Heb. 1:1-3 KJV)

A general survey of the category of revelation and reflections upon the definitive disclosure of God's essential person in Jesus Christ, the brightest star in the constellation of revelation are essential starting points. The uniqueness of the biblical narrative that culminates in the Christ event is the context for consideration of the challenge of plausibility while preaching amidst the diversity of truth claims in a pluralistic age. The implications of this were brought home to me in a sobering way at a George Barna Seminar I attended some years ago of which the theme was <u>Leading Your Church Forward</u>. Barna estimated that only 9 percent of born again adults have a biblical worldview. In addition, only 15 percent of born again adults have the foundation or theological perspective needed for a biblical worldview.[1] Barna's astounding, relevant and sobering critique focused on three areas: (1) belief in absolute moral truth, (2) belief that the Bible is the standard of moral truth and (3) core religious beliefs that conform to biblical teaching in the areas of the nature and existence of God, the sinless life of Jesus Christ, the existence of Satan, the ability to earn salvation, personal responsibility of sharing the Gospel and the reliability of Scripture.

These practical and paradigmatic considerations have grave implications for preaching. Why should the people take seriously what the preacher-pastor says when there are so many voices and visions vying for their allegiance? Like some Jacob at Jabbok, the concerned and committed pastor must wrestle with these fundamental issues while considering the effectiveness of preaching to cast, clarify and communicate the mission and vision of the local church.

John Stott strikes at the very heart of this issue. Concerning revelation and the urgency to preach the Gospel, he says:

> It is a basic tenet of the Christian religion that we believe what we believe because God has revealed it. In consequence, there is an authority in Christianity which can never be destroyed. Preachers who share this assurance see themselves as trustees of divine revelation, or, as the apostle Paul expressed it, "stewards of the mysteries of God" (1 Cor. 4:1), that is, of the secrets which he has disclosed ... it will enable us to proclaim the gospel with quiet confidence as good news from God.[2]

*Can Man Live Without God?*, the title of the signal work by noted Christian apologist, Dr. Ravi Zacharias raises a pointed and timely issue for those who preach. He asserts that it is Jesus who gives wonder, meaning and coherence to human existence.[3] In the wilderness Jesus, as Satan himself tempted him, boldly negated any presupposition that ultimate happiness and fulfillment could be actualized in merely a physical and material realm alone. Jesus responded to the Tempter with an affirmation that is at the core of our unique essence, "It is written, Man shall not live by bread alone, but by every word that proceedeth out of the mouth of God" (Matt. 4:4b KJV). In every instance during the temptation, Jesus rebuffed Satan's advances by quoting from the Old Testament scriptures. The greatest preacher that ever lived carried His Bible into battle! When He could have summoned the stars in the sky, the ocean in its depths or the angelic hosts to the defense, He chose to elevate and punctuate the Word of God.

And what a Word it is! In an age and culture that decries absolute truth and anything that symbolizes authority, sound preaching in the pastorate must be persistently predicated on the supernaturally revealed, divinely inspired and infallible Word of God. This is both the center and the circumference of biblical preaching. God has exhaled the life giving and life-sustaining words that animate and motivate

Christian worship, witness, work and warfare. "All scripture is given by inspiration of God, and is profitable for doctrine, for reproof, for correction, for instruction in righteousness that the man of God may be perfect, thoroughly furnished unto all good works" (2 Tim. 3:16 KJV).

The efficacy of Jeremiah's prophetic ministry was rooted and grounded in the assurance he received during his call that God had taken the initiative. With words that inspire and encourage every preacher he says, "Then the Lord put forth his hand, and touched my mouth. And the Lord said unto me, "Behold I have put my words in thy mouth" (Jer. 1:9 KJV). The preacher's calling is predicated on the reality that God has already spoken with authority and the transmission of God's speech or words with integrity and consistency is the preacher's primary responsibility. Those who transact in this sacred business today must launch this enterprise from the infallible and inspired Word of God as recorded in the Scriptures.

If the pulpit falls prey to the purveyors of an errant subjectivism or a misguided humanism, preaching loses its voice and vitality. We have no words apart from the supernatural and inspired Word that comes from God. John Stott outlines an appropriate Christian response to this "anti-authority" mood in our culture.

> But suppose in our preaching we are careful to demonstrate that the authority which we preach inheres neither in us as individuals, nor primarily in our office as clergy or preachers, nor even in the church whose members and accredited pastors we may be, but supremely in the Word of God which we expound? Then the people should be willing to hear, particularly if we put the matter beyond doubt by showing that we desire to live under this authority ourselves.[4]

We must then preach presupposing that biblical revelation is God's response to the contingent and paradoxical nature of human existence. Dietrich Bonhoeffer was right — "God is not the limits of life but the Centre." In revelation, God has staged and launched an invasion, a coup de tat that is truly good news, offers everlasting life, vibrant with potentiality and yet inexhaustible in mystery. God's activity requires a faith response on our part. This is the goal of biblical preaching. The pastor-teacher committed to caring for conflicted and confused congregants and armed with the supernatural Word of God purposes to comfort the disturbed and disturb the comfortable. The late Dr. Paul Scherer called this an "imperative indicative." But our faith response to the reality of God's revelation is not merely assent to dogma or creed but rather the attitude of an acknowledged insufficiency met by the sufficiency of God which can be experienced in personal relationship.

C. Stephen Evans argues that God has left calling cards or clues that center on three fundamental mysteries — the mystery of the universe, the mystery of the moral order and the mystery of human personhood.[5] As regards, human personhood, God has left a God-shaped hole in us that only God can fill; an insatiable need that compels us to reach beyond our contingencies in search of eternal life, eternal meaning and eternal love.[6] Saint Augustine said, "My heart is restless until it finds its rest in Thee." This resembles the magnificent musings of the Psalmist who says, "As the hart panteth after the water brooks, so panteth my soul after thee, O God (Ps. 42:1 KJV). The culture of modernity mocks the significance of this search binding those who peddle and purchase its pernicious poison into virtual prisons of subjectivity and subjugation to the sensory and the secular.

Some years ago, I attended a preaching conference in Dallas. My wife and I drove from Georgetown, Kentucky to Dallas, Texas, approximately nine hundred miles. Before the age of GPS, I requested a trip ticket from my travel club that they promptly provided. It was detailed with maps, guides, mileage estimates, points of interests, and recommendations well-being. In essence, preaching Christ and Him crucified is the <u>only</u> alternative for those that have lost their way in the maze and malaise of self-centeredness, sin and suffering.

Therefore, the <u>Truth</u> that has been ultimately revealed and fulfilled in Christ must be incarnated anew in the lives of the audience so that it becomes the only truth that matters. The preacher is not only a courier but a conduit and catalyst as well. This has been and is the essence and genius of the best in Black preaching and is at the heart of the pastor's task.

CHAPTER 4

# Preaching and Mission Holism - Part 1

Upon beginning pastoral duties at the First Baptist Church, Chesterfield, Missouri on February 6, 2000, it was obvious that there were two major pastoral challenges. First, I was faced with the challenge of energizing the leadership with a clear sense of direction and accountability. Secondly, there was an urgent need to galvanize the congregation around a central theme and focus while embracing the stated mission and vision of the church. During the pastoral vacancy an intentional interim process was implemented. During this process, the congregation adopted a revised mission and vision statement. The mission statement states:

> The mission of this church is to advance the Kingdom of Jesus Christ in accordance to Matthew 28:18-20 through preaching of the Gospel, consistent Christian living, personal evangelism, missionary endeavor, Christian education and the public worship of God.
> (First Baptist Church of Chesterfield 1999)

The companion vision statement states:

> The First Baptist Church of Chesterfield will move "Forward in Faith" emulating the work of

our Lord and Savior Jesus Christ, ministering to all people by exalting the Savior, equipping and supporting the members for ministry and evangelizing the lost while continuing to nourish our rich cultural heritage. (First Baptist Church of Chesterfield 1999)

I prayerfully ascribed to these statements as a pastoral candidate, recognizing the vision statement needed greater specificity and clarity in order to provide a clear and cogent picture of what the church will look like as the mission is actualized. Over the years this amplification has occurred through specific interventions and strategic initiatives that concretized the vision and mission for the church and propelled the ministry forward and outward. For example, at a key planning workshop with church leaders, the vision statement was modified a few years ago with the phrase, "while continuing to nourish our rich *Christian* and cultural heritage" to signal our commitment as a spiritual community to being "exclusively inclusive."

As the First Baptist Church of Chesterfield continues to move from biblical message to vision and mission actualization, the congregation embraces a unique distinctiveness as a historic, predominantly African-American congregation in the fast growing and affluent West County region of greater metropolitan St. Louis, Missouri. The immediate actualization of the vision in this ministry periphery and environment necessitates the ongoing need to affirm our racial, cultural and ethnic heritage while engaging the greater urgency of advancing the kingdom of God in a community that is predominantly white and white collar.

Therefore, the task and essential commitment to mission embraced by any local congregation necessitates solid biblical and theological foundations. This is the locus on which the superstructure of a mission focus must be erected. Therefore, the pastor adorns the garb of a missionologist in order to engage critical biblical and theological issues related to missions. This occurs with a clear recognition that there is inherent and negative entropy in established and historic institutions that causes them to turn inward rather than outward. Thomas Rainer observes, "The very nature of a vision is that it leads a church to a point beyond the status quo. Such a process always engenders change. Resistance to change is common to churches that have been in a familiar and comfortable pattern".[1] Consequently, apart from any prayerful, thoughtful, and intentional impetus in the opposite direction, ministry tends to be primarily centripetal rather than centrifugal.

CHAPTER 5

# Preaching and Mission Holism

## PART 2

### PREACHING AND THE MISSION OF GOD

The starting point for any discussion of the relationship between preaching and holism in Christian mission or missions is crucial. Rather than launching from a sociological praxis in his treatment of the biblical foundations of missions, George Peters insists on a theocentric approach. He notes, "Theocentric missions find its source, dynamic, and goal beyond time and space in eternity, though it does not bypass current history. Time, however, cannot originate, sustain or exhaust it".[1] Peters concludes his treatment with a thoughtful assessment of God's triune engagement in the missionary endeavor.

We may conclude that the triune God whose very essence is Spirit, light and love is an outgoing God. God is a missionary God, initiating benevolent relations to all humanity, ever searching in love to bestow blessings on all, and even offering the Son as a vicarious sacrifice to make our salvation possible. Father, Son and Holy Spirit are cooperating and coordinating to bring us back from our sinful wandering and blundering, and restoring us to a pristine state, purpose, destiny and glory.[2] According to Scripture, the phalanx of God's redemptive activity is the preaching of the cross of Christ. The content of the message was viewed with cynicism and skepticism by the cultural and intellectual elite of the New Testament world. The fact that this powerful, life changing message was and still is cloaked and clothed in the frail and flawed fragility of the messenger exacerbates this holy hilarity (see 1 Cor. 1:21; 2 Cor. 4:7).

George Peter's "missionary God" invades and acts in human history and redemption in triune particularity. This is significant in light of the philosophical and theological traditions in church history that reduced the doctrine of the trinity to abstract and sterile monotheism. These traditions erroneously represent the triune God either as a homogeneous divine substance or one identical divine subject. God's pathos for Israel anticipates the suffering of the Son, Jesus Christ. God is not impassive but passionately committed to redeeming creature and creation and, in Trinitarian differentiation, goes out of God's self and becomes actively involved in the world (see Phil. 2:5-11).

Therefore, the perspective from which the preacher and pastor views the nature of God is determinative for *missio Dei* or the mission of God. The mission of God finds its origin in the heart of God.[3] Mission is a challenge to God's essence and not God's existence. It is urgent then that a vision or theology of God that is loving, inclusive and inviting bolsters holism in Christian missions.

The dogged determination of the Divine to redeem creature and creation is manifest throughout the scriptures. Listen to Jeremiah's words to Israel, "For I know the thoughts that I think toward you, saith the LORD, thoughts of peace, and not of evil, to give you an expected end" (Jer. 29:11 KJV). Equally arresting are the words of the prophet Hosea on God's behalf to apostate Israel, "I led Israel along with my ropes of kindness and love. I lifted the yoke from his neck, and I myself stooped to feed him (Hos. 11:4 NLT).

A similar theme resonates in Peter's declaration to the church. "The Lord is not slack concerning his promise, as some men count slackness; but is longsuffering to us-ward, not willing that any should perish, but that all should come to repentance" (2 Pet. 3.9 KJV).

The opening chapters of the Bible reveal God as the One who enters into relationship with the creation. Chris Wright is right to posit the creation platform as the foundations of missions. He says, "A biblical basis for missions must begin with the creation platform because it provides the basic biblical world-view of reality: God, the earth, and humanity in reciprocal relation to each other".[4] In the New Testament, the eternality of Jesus Christ is attested by His involvement in creation. Ultimately though, it is the incarnation of God in the historical person of Jesus Christ that represents the decisive moment in the revelatory constellation (see Heb. 1:1-3). It is the incarnation interface, this unprecedented point of particularity where all that is God-ness and goodness engages our human frailty, finitude and fragmentation. It is this sphere of a sacred specificity, God's pathos and redemptive identification with humanity in our sufferings that is anticipated in God's unique covenantal relationship with Israel. Therefore, creation can be viewed from the social-human context in that it is not so much concerned with origins but rather with human freedom and the renewal and liberation of human life. Israel becomes then the context and conduit for the dynamic of God at work in human existence. To this glorious end and purpose the prophets and seers of the Old Testament directed their proclamations.

Anticipating the formalizing of a covenant relationship with Israel, it is interesting that in a poignant prelude on Mount Sinai, God summons Moses from the midst of a bush that burned but did not consume. At this point of Moses's commissioning as the Lawgiver of Israel, God reveals God's essential Self as "I am that I am" (See Exod. 3:14 KJV). It is significant that this ontological reality and declaration was given to Moses the preacher, prophet and liberator as the precedent and preparation for any experiential engagement of the plight of the oppressed Israelites. The tumultuous struggle that ensued in Egypt and which began with Moses's initial confrontation of an oppressive Pharaoh was prefaced with these words,

> The LORD God of the Hebrews hath sent me unto thee, saying, Let my people go, that they may serve me in the wilderness: and, behold, hitherto thou wouldest not hear. Thus saith the LORD, In this thou shalt know that I am the LORD: behold, I will smite with the rod that is in mine hand upon the waters which are in the river, and they shall be turned to blood. (Exod. 7:16-17 KJV)

The implications are clear that it is in the context of missions, the preacher becomes part of a God project which aims to mitigate sin and suffering in this world by bringing others into a true knowledge of the One whose image we bear. The result is that unbelievers will come to know that the God of Israel who is the Father of our Lord Jesus Christ, the Head of the church, is the One True God. The holistic nature of God's redemption of Israel can only be understood in light of God's timeless intent to vindicate and validate God's true essence in the context of human sin and suffering. In the Genesis narrative, the Father commands everything that ever will be to exist, the Spirit broods over the formless and empty chaos, and the Son walks through the Garden to confront man and woman in their existential estrangement. Creation anticipates our redemption as much as redemption reflects the fulfillment of God's intent and design for all persons. The Apostle Paul reminded the Colossians of this great truth. "For by him were all things created, that are in heaven, and that are in earth, visible and invisible, whether they be thrones, or dominions, or principalities, or powers: all things were created by him, and for him" (Col. 1:16 KJV). This reality is the essential impetus and imperative for the Christian mission to the world and the inviting incentive for the preacher's task.

## PREACHING AND THE MISSION OF THE CHURCH

The purposefulness of God's engagement of the social-human context through the ministry of preaching has to do with its determinative and normative significance for the mission of the church or what is called *missiones ecclesiarium*. Like Israel, the church exists in unique relationship with God. This relationship in both instances has vertical and horizontal polarities. The relationship to God can best be described as priestly with a focus on worship while the relationship to others is ambassadorial with a focus on witness. This dual commission is explicit in John's prelude to the *Book of Revelation*, "And hath made us kings and priests unto God and his Father; to him be glory and dominion for ever and ever. Amen" (Rev. 1:6 KJV) (see also 1 Pet. 2:9).

The message and ministry of Jesus who came preaching emerges in this exclusive milieu and is anticipated by God's unique call and election of Israel. In the Gospels, the mission motif is more implicit than explicit. The kingdom of Jesus has an implicit universal dimension and is an expansive image of God, an inclusive view of God's people, and a positive view of human destiny.[5]

Jesus does not give the church a full-blown mission strategy but rather lays the foundation for the church's post-resurrection mission activity. Jesus' primary mission strategy is not a detailed plan but dedicated persons of whom He is the model and mentor. This dedication and determination is energized by the indwelling and filling of the Holy Spirit (see Acts 1:8). Jesus anticipated the enabling ministry of the Holy Spirit because he did not only ordain the apostles but He set them aside to be <u>with Him</u> (see Mark 3:14).

Another example is the Apostle Paul who was first and foremost a preacher and pastor. Energized by the transforming trauma of his own conversion, he became a tremendous force for missions in the life of the early church. It is the confluence of sources that shaped Paul's mission theology, which makes his contribution significant.

Most importantly was his understanding of the history and mission of Israel and the provisional nature of the Law and priestly cult. Through Paul's tireless efforts, the church became truly cosmopolitan. Paul's letters are primarily pastoral, but provide a healthy, wholesome pragmatism for the development of mission theology in the context of the contemporary church. This is the focus of an important passage in First Thessalonians. "For from you sounded out the word of the Lord not only in Macedonia and Achaia, but also in every place your faith to God-ward is spread abroad; so that we need not to speak any thing" (1 Thess. 1:8 KJV). Their receptivity of the Gospel message had implications well beyond the local congregation.

It is significant to remember that Paul understood the history of Israel was an example to those that believe. "Now all these things happened unto them for ensamples: and they are written for our admonition, upon whom the ends of the world are come" (1 Cor. 10:11 KJV). In Colossians, the lordship of Jesus Christ is positioned on the creation platform and extends to the universal mission of the church.

## PREACHING AND THE MISSION OF THE PASTOR-TEACHER

My grasp and gasp of the immensity of the calling, character and craft of the pastor-teacher as preacher has been reconfigured, recalibrated and reenergized by this opportunity to share my experiences with a larger audience. I am like some David standing awestruck in the lengthening shadow of the massive sculpture Michelangelo carved and crafted in his honor and memory. Spirit-empowered, Bible centered preaching is a spiritual entity; it's God's idea and God's property. While transacted in the context of the church's life and mission, preaching is ultimately transcendent. The preached word comes "from the Lord." Like some Isaiah, confronting the transcendent, thunderous vision of

God's holiness in the Temple, this project ushered the writer repeatedly into the glare and gaze of the Holy where he was reminded again and again that "... we have this treasure in earthen vessels" (2 Cor. 4:7 KJV).

The eminent preacher, pastor and hymnologist Phillips Brooks defined preaching as the "communication of truth by men to men." It has in it two essential elements, truth and personality".[6] While the truth is pure, heavenly and supernatural, the carrier and conduit is flawed. George Rogers describes preaching as an "impossible possibility." He continues by noting,

> Yet, if preaching is not a human possibility, responsive to our techniques and mastery, it is a divine possibility in which God may, and does, engage his church, and certain men and women therein, as earthen vessels for carrying forth and pouring out into the world the treasure of the gospel.[7]

Yet Paul accentuated the centrality of the preacher's task as it relates to the purposes of God who, "... hath in due times manifested his word through preaching, which is committed unto me according to the commandment of God our Savior" (Titus 1:3 KJV). The late Dr. Gardner Taylor, Pastor Emeritus of the Concord Baptist Church, Brooklyn, New York, and long adored as a prince of preachers in the African American faith tradition, argues that at the heart of this hilarity, the foolishness of preaching is its utter presumptuousness. With remarkable insight Taylor says,

> The person who preaches is as guilty of the wrongs against God against which he inveighs as are those to whom he addresses his words. He cannot help feeling deep embarrassment at the recognition that those who hear are likely

> to ask justifiably, "Who is he to talk? Listen to her! Can you imagine the nerve?" God help the preacher who is so self-hypnotized that the full brunt of this shame does not fall like an awful weight upon him, loading what he says with a becoming humility and hush of the soul that he, of all people, should be sent to say such things about what is wrong with people before God. For what is wrong with the hearers is the same that is wrong with the preacher.[8]

A critical and cohesive discussion of preaching and the ministry of the pastor-teacher must engage not only the content of the preacher's communication but the reality of the preacher as one called and consecrated to spiritual service. The spirituality of the preacher, or the lack of it, advances or impedes the communication of the truth. "Take heed unto thyself, and unto the doctrine; continue in them: for in doing this thou shalt both save thyself, and them that hear thee" (1 Tim. 4:16 KJV).

The supernatural truth, which ought to be the preacher's compelling object and constant obsession, cannot be revised or revamped. Preaching epitomizes as nothing else in Christian ministry what has been called "the two sides of the great human contradiction, dust and divinity".[9]

The interface between preaching, the mission of God and the mission of the church is the unique calling and character of the preacher as a spiritual person. A spiritual person is one who is integrated into the rule of God. What is the impact of this ongoing integration on the preacher's sense of call, the character of the preacher and the craft of preaching?

In a classic passage that is considered by many to be the call of Jeremiah to the prophetic ministry, God reminds the prophet to be that his call has both post-natal and pre-natal implications. "Before I formed thee in the belly I knew thee; and before thou camest forth out of the womb I sanctified thee, and I ordained thee a prophet unto the nations" (Jer. 1:5 KJV). In my faith tradition, it is often said that "you don't pick preaching up; preaching picks you up." The preacher must be borne to preaching by an abiding, unshakable sense of divine call. However this is actuated in the preacher's experience, it is a prerequisite to proclaiming the Word of God. The preacher is accosted by God in the inner self. The consciousness of divine calling gives birth to a resolute tenacity that affirms unequivocally as did the Apostle Paul, "For though I preach the gospel, I have nothing to glory of: necessity is laid upon me; yea, woe is unto me, if I preach not the gospel" (1 Cor. 9:16 KJV). James Gordon asserts that the experience of grace, God's initiative, is at the very center of evangelical Christianity. The recognition of God's grace frames and fuels the responsiveness of the recipient. He says:

> Grace, then is not a comfortable word; if it announces free forgiving love it also intimates the moral demand of an infinite obligation placed on the redeemed heart ... Each Christian seeking to live the life of grace derives energy and the will to obedience from the creative fusion in the heart of inexplicable blessing in Christ, profound indebtedness, and grateful adoration. Spirituality includes amongst its deepest motives the glad obedience and disciplined gratitude of worshipping love.[10]

This divine initiative is the grace of God operative in the preacher's life. None is worthy and God is not so impoverished in that God needs human instruments to do God's will. Therefore, at the very outset, the call to preach is shrouded in contradiction. Those who preach must approach this holy vocation with a humbling awareness of their spiritual bankruptcy and irreparable unworthiness. The preacher is spiritually

## ETHOS, PATHOS AND LOGOS

The classic divisions of ancient Greek rhetoric are <u>ethos</u>, <u>pathos</u> and <u>logos</u>. These were considered to be the three primary modes of persuasion. These categories facilitate an understanding of preaching as it relates to the role, function and character of the pastor.

<u>Ethos</u> has to do with the character of the messenger. It can be expressed both by the lifestyle of the messenger and the content of the message. <u>Pathos</u> lies in the audience; what they believe, want and desire; what issues are impactful and significant for them. <u>Logos</u> has to do with the content of the message; the authority and power vested in the content especially the power of the symbolic. For the Christian preacher, <u>ethos</u> begins with the action of the Holy Spirit in both regeneration and the call experience. Regeneration and the call to preach are tantamount to what the poet described as "a presence that disturbs me with the joy of elevated thoughts" (William Wordsworth).

The ordinary events of life provide the basis for <u>pathos</u> in ministry. God endorses the preacher's candidacy for the trials and tribulations of life that the preacher can grow spiritually but also connect and empathize with the suffering of others. Brother Lawrence is helpful:

> That when we enter the spiritual life we should consider in depth who we are, and then we will find we are deserving of all contempt, unworthy of the name Christian, subject to all kinds of miseries and to countless accidents ... whom God must humble with an infinite variety of sufferings and travail, within as well as without ... Should we not, on the contrary submit to these sufferings and bear them as long as God wishes us to as things which are to our advantage.[16]

Certainly, one of the advantages is the ability to relate, to be compassionate to those to whom our preachments are directed.

Some years ago because of enhancements on the church's computer, I purchased an adapter for the computer's keyboard. Each end of the adapter was unique and distinct. One end fitted for the processing unit and the other for the keyboard connect. So it is in Christian ministry, our adaptation requires a right relationship to God (this I call verticality) and a right relationship to others (horizontality). Our community with others, especially as we experience fraternity and sorority with their sufferings are predicated on our community with Christ. Consequently, "... we may well be able to comfort them which are in any trouble, by the comfort wherewith we ourselves are comforted of God" (2 Cor. 1:4 KJV). Henry Mitchell relates this relational mutuality and reciprocity to the preaching task. He says,

> The Black preacher must be ear deep in the condition of the people, and out of this comes the easy dialogue between the preacher and the people, whose lives are intimately close together — so close together that the themes which invade the consciousness of the one also invades the others.[17]

Finally, Logos provides the content of preaching as the preacher and pastor through the intimacy encouraged by the spiritual disciplines mimics and models the life and death of the Lord Jesus Christ. Every sermon must be rooted in the intimacy of this gaze and gait. Logos is the nectar, or what Brother Lawrence calls, the "inexpressible sweetness" which we taste as we nurse on the breasts of God[18]. Spiritual life is the ability to reach out to God (the result of God reaching down to us) and through Him, to others. We don't reach around God to others but through Him. Preaching is conceived in the womb of the preacher's intimacy with God and then born into the world of others. Because of this character, preaching is necessarily both theocentric and anthropocentric.

The character transformation that is prerequisite to and ongoing in the preaching of the Word of God takes place through purposed intention of the preacher to bring personality and one's total being into effective cooperation with the divine order.[19] What is pocketed initially in the privacy of the preacher's priesthood before God, ends in the corporeity of the church's experience.

George A. Lane's *Christian Spirituality*, is a helpful and informative survey of the history of Christian spirituality with a primary focus on the monastic traditions. Based on his analysis, there are striking parallels between the eremitic, coenobitic and mendicant monastic lifestyles and the cultivation of spirituality.[20] Authentic spirituality evolves in the solitude of our desert experiences, the interrelations of the faith community and is launched inevitably in mission and message to the world. These monastic traditions speak to the various spheres where character transformation evolves in the life of the preacher.

CHAPTER 6

# The pastor as change agent

Calling and character, nurtured by a humbling sense of grace and giftedness, and strengthened by the practice of the disciplines is the foundation from which the craft of preaching is launched, the pastoral task executed, and the kingdom of God concretized in the life of the local church. This is the foundation on which the superstructure of ministry is erected as saints are equipped for the work of the ministry and the local congregation is edified to the glory of God. It is also the non-negotiable prerequisite for any pastor committed to effectively leading change and transition in the local church and moving a congregation toward the actualization of mission and vision. To what extent does the credibility of the message and the messenger impact and relate to change and transition in the local church?

This analysis and delineation of the pastoral task, while maintaining an immediate focus on preaching, is also the record and results of a pastor's leadership in a crucial area of ministry. The story is told of a pastor whose leadership was being challenged by a disruptive and disorderly deacon. With some frustration the pastor responded to the criticism by saying, "My God given responsibility as pastor is to lead and to feed." The deacon responded, "I guess my job is to follow and swallow!"

While this story is quite humorous, it does accentuate the irrevocable union between the pastor's role as a communicator of the Word of God and the pastor's role as leader. These are two things the Lord has truly joined together. Pastoral preaching casts, communicates and clarifies the mission and vision of the local congregation which is seeded, soldered and seared in the prayerful heart of God's servant by the Holy Spirit. The effective actualization of this lofty charge and challenge necessitates prayerful and intentional leadership on the part of the pastor while building in the congregation a cooperative and inclusive foundation for transition and transformation. Therefore, let's turn our focus to the critical role the pastor plays as a change agent while moving the congregation toward an envisioned destination.

The pastor's leadership when proactively and courageously inclusive will greatly encourage and expedite the process of ongoing renewal and revitalization in the congregation. Someone said, "If you are leading and no one is following, you are only taking a walk". Servant leadership encourages others to become a part of the solution and not the problem. Such leadership is empowering and enabling. In his book, *Dying for Change*, Leith Anderson says,

> The renewing of the church ... must be bound by the cause of Jesus Christ but open to new ideas and changing structures. Distinction must be made between moral absolutes and cultural relatives. Yesterday's answers are not always appropriate for today's questions. Change and challenge should not be threatening but recognized as part of the process. Leaders must keep calling the organization and its people back to the Lordship of Jesus Christ and the standards of the Bible while challenging

people to grow and innovate within the biblical boundaries. Fulfilling the mission is always more important than perpetuating traditions.[1]

Building on a distinction that Lyle Schaller makes between <u>transactional</u> and <u>transformational</u> leaders, Leith Anderson makes a very convincing argument for the necessity of leaders initiating change to recognize the difference between power and authority. He says,

> At this point it is important to distinguish between authority and power. Power is holding a gun to a person's head or withholding a paycheck from an employee. Power forces others to obey, even against their wills. Authority is earned. Authority is freely given. Authority is people listening to and acting on the words of a leader because they choose to and want to. Authority is trust and confidence. Not understanding the difference and assuming authority that has not been given is a certain route to disaster in a church or an organization.[2]

Anderson provides a sobering reminder that whatever the initiative, the pastor must never forget that the church is a body unity and that leaders and followers are defined and determined just as much by their interdependence as by their individuality. Paul said, "For as the body is one, and hath many members, and all the members of that one body, being many, are one body so also is Christ" (1 Cor. 12:12 KJV). To forget either the body or its parts can be catastrophic. C. S. Lewis characterizes this quality as it relates to our moral nature and obligations in his book *Mere Christianity*. He notes,

> You can get the idea plain if you think of us as a fleet of ships sailing in formation. The

> voyage will be a success only, in the first place, if the ships do not collide and get in one another's way; and, secondly, if each ship is seaworthy and her engines in good order. As a matter of fact, you cannot have either of these two things without the other.[3]

Lasting change must be purposive, intentional and deliberate and, as we have already seen, bolstered on solid biblical and theological foundations. Such intention shields the shepherd and the sheep from bogus expectations and the always potentially disabling and disastrous distractions of ministry. Because of the contentious and conflicted environment in which Christian ministry is transacted, it is important that we communicate not only "Whose" we are, who we are but also why we are. Strategic focus and grasp of the big picture fortresses the leader from the dangerous, devilish and diabolical seductions of pleasure, power and parade.[4]

Beyond theological conviction, planned, purposeful change and transition in the local church must be informed by the pastor's sociological awareness of the local congregational setting and psychological insight into how group dynamics encourage or impede the ability of persons to act. Effective change and transition require that leadership interventions be thoughtful and purposive. A mental construct or map is the precedent and priority that encourages confidence, receptivity and ownership. Doug Murren emphasizes the importance of a thoughtful plan in a discussion about the key ingredients of change.

> Finally, change requires insight. A group considering the acceptance of change requires a leader who is credible and trustworthy. If the followers believe that their leader has created a workable plan, the chances that the leader seeing

the change through to implementation is greatly improved. The people however, are not likely to give permission to make a significant change unless they first have hard evidence of a well-conceived strategy for making things better.[5]

The "meta-strategies" of leading, proclaiming, and caring are all essential components every wise and effective pastor leverages while establishing credibility and ownership for the vision and mission of the local church.[6] These three strategies are interconnected and form the golden triangle that defines and shapes the ongoing pastoral priority and process that provide boundaries, establish priorities and create the context for the receptivity and implementation of the preached word in ministry and mission.

In his typically distinctive and dynamic delineations and declarations, my mentor, the late Dr. Manuel Scott, Sr., provides compelling clarity about the point and place where these pastoral priorities collide, corroborate and coalesce. In his classic treatise on preaching, *From A Black Brother*, he writes,

> "Whatever else may be the goal of the preacher's proclamation, it aims, essentially at changing things as they are and converting them into things as they ought to be. He speaks in the unmitigated optimism that no man needs to stay the way he is and that no condition has immunity against change. To make the rough places smooth, to exalt the valleys and level mountains, to build highways and desert places, to set at liberty those who are bound, to restore hearing to the deaf and to recover sight for the blind, and

> to shine a light for those who walk in darkness and dwell in the regions of the shadows, are among the preacher's top task and intrigues".[7]

Scott and Stubblefield share a similar passion and perspective. Pastoral preaching is not an isolated island but a a sprawling continent of possibility tapestried and textured with mountains and valleys, lakes and rivers, and meadows and deserts. Whatever form these geographic markers assume in pastoral ministry and congregational life, they are never just obstacles or oases but opportunities for radical redemption and transformative change.

So let us turn now to Part 2 and survey a more detailed delineation of these transformative strategies as we consider the missional wave that propels the ministry when the pastor-teacher prayerfully, purposely and passionately engages the local congregation as a servant-leader.

PART 2

# RIDING THE WAVE
## THE PASTOR AS SERVANT-LEADER

CHAPTER 7

# THE GREATEST AMONG YOU

The word *leader* occurs in the Bible just three (3) times. But the word *servant* occurs four-hundred eight (480) times. This stark contrast of biblical emphasis speaks profoundly to something very fundamental about the role of the pastor as leader. The pastor is primarily a "servant-leader." We lead by serving others. The way up is down - servanthood is the divinely determined downward descent to upward mobility in ministry. See Phil. 2:1ff. This is the signature and singular note that every pastor must set or the rest of the pastoral song will be out of tune. I share this with you at a time in the contemporary church when malignant elitism and misplaced egotism haunts, hobbles and hurts too many who are called by God to be purveyors of the Cross, proclaimers of the Truth and protectors of the Sheep.

I remember as a new pastor at the First Baptist Church of Georgetown, Kentucky working alongside the men of the church on a number of long overdue building and grounds projects aimed to improve and spice up the general appearance of an aging facility. I soon became aware that adorning work clothes, using hammer, nail and saw, scraping old paint away and applying a new coat, or pushing a wheelbarrow laden with rock and gravel could greatly enhance and enlarge my pastoral capital with leaders and members. This principle is much like the engineer of the locomotive that often places the train's powerful engine in reverse in order to attach to the load and then roar, roll and rumble forward toward the appointed destination.

Unprincipled entitlement and unchecked egotism are pernicious piranhas that will marginalize, minimize and maroon a church or ministry in mediocrity. This is not the model that our Lord demonstrated. Jesus's emphatic edict and extraordinary example is timeless. He said to both his disciples and his detractors, "And whoever of you wants to be first must be your slave; for the Son of man himself has not come to be served but to serve, and to give his life as a ransom for many" (Mark 10:44-45 Moffatt). The Supreme Servant sacrificed for those whom He loved. How climatically fitting that at the Last Supper, He took off his outer garment, adorned a towel and, with basin in hand moved around the table where the disciples reclined and washed their feet. We ride the wave created by His supreme example when we commit above all else to serving others. The pastor cannot be needy, seedy or greedy!

There is a scene in the 1987 crime drama, *The Untouchables* that is riveting and revealing. Set in the Prohibition Era, the beat cop Jim Malone played by actor Sean Connery is meeting with Eliot Ness played by Kevin Costner. Their interaction takes place in the ornate sanctuary of a church. Ness, an FBI agent recently assigned to lead a task force to combat organized crime in Chicago, is seeking to recruit Malone as a member of his elite team of agents who will have in their sights an all-out assault on the titular head of organized crime in the city, the vicious and violent gang leader Al Capone.

Malone, a devout Catholic in the movie shares a memorable scene with Ness while both are bowed on bended knees in the church's sanctuary. As he grips and gyrates a rosary with his hands, Malone reminds Ness that the Chicago police know where Capone keeps his liquor, who buys it and how and when it is distributed. The challenge that none in law enforcement has been willing to accept is to go and get it. Then Malone asks the question, "What are you willing to do?" In others words, what are you willing to give up in order to reach your goal? The noted playwright Oscar Wilde said, "Life imitates art and art life." I ask my pastoral and ministry colleagues who truly desire to ride the wave Jesus set in motion and lead your people from message to mission, what are you willing to do?

Pastor, author and leadership expert Dr. John Maxwell has blessed me over the years with his insights on this subject. In his excellent book *Twenty-One Irrefutable Laws of Leadership*, he shares about the leader's lid or "The Law of the Lid". He writes,

> "I believe that success is within the reach of just about everyone. But I also believe that personal success without leadership ability brings only limited effectiveness. A person's impact is only a fraction of what it could be with good leadership. The higher you want to climb, the more you need leadership. The greater the impact you want to make, the greater your influence needs to be. Whatever you will accomplish is restricted to your ability to lead others".[1]

Leadership capacity is synonymous with the leader's ceiling or lid. In ministry, a leader's lid level is established ultimately by his or her capacity and commitment to lifting others. I remember attending a banquet a few years ago; a service organization in the community sponsored it. I still remember the sign behind the dais that read, "As you climb, lift!" Since then, those words have been etched indelibly in my consciousness. As I climb, as you climb, who are we lifting? A wise person once said to me, "Everyone should be engaged in three types of relationships. You need a Paul to walk in front of you, a Barnabas to walk alongside you and a Timothy to walk behind you."

Dr. Earnest O. White was my professor at Southern Baptist Theological Seminary in Louisville, Kentucky. He taught a class on "The Ministry of Leadership." In his excellent book on the subject, *Becoming a Christian Leader*, he notes that leadership is informed by the variables of task, relationship, servanthood and authority. While task and relationship are common themes in the broad field of management theory, Dr. White affirmed and accentuated more than once the timeless and uniqueness of servanthood and authority for the Christian leader. Servant leadership launches from the axis of human need and is conceptually modeled and mirrored in the shepherd image so common to Jesus's teaching".[2] Robert Dale in his book, *Pastoral Leadership* argues that "a starting point for Christian leaders is an examination of the leader stance and style of Jesus. Servanthood is the basic image of the person and work of Christ".[3]

While walking on the beach one day, I asked a surfer what the long cord was called that was attached to his leg and the surfboard. He said, "It is called a *leash* so that a surfer will never lose connection to the board. Unleashed, the board pushed along by the force of the waves could be a danger to him or others."

Well, Jesus in His earthly ministry was tied and tethered to the board called servanthood. Ultimately, He laid His life down allowing the Jewish and Roman authorities to nail Him to the Cross of Calvary in order to save us from our sins. From the beginning of His ministry, that was what He was prepared to do! What about you?

CHAPTER 8

# DIAGNOSING AND ENGAGING THE CONGREGATIONAL CULTURE

What is culture? Every organization has it! Every local church has it! Understanding the culture of a local congregation and the resultant sense of community, continuity and connectivity they create are integral in not only initiating change but resolving conflict. Culture is the patterned ways in which people relate. Doctors and scientists extract a "culture" in order to evaluate patients, diagnose and treat disease or monitor experiments for scientific research. Dr. Charles Kraft in his book *Christianity in Culture* states, "Humans thus may be regarded as culture-shaped and culture-transforming beings. But we not only are shaped by and participate in the transmission of our culture; we also influence it and contribute to its reshaping".[1]

This observation should challenge and encourage pastors who are called not only to be different but to make a difference wherever God places them. As I approach the end of twenty years of pastoral ministry in my present role, I am greatly encouraged by the cultural transformation that has taken place at the First Baptist Church of Chesterfield. We have evolved from "the little church on the side of the hill", a small, inwardly focused family church to a missional congregation that provides consistent support to a number of local, regional, national and international organizations and churches. We have by God's grace successfully navigated the tenuous tensions and risky rapids that every congregation faces during a pastoral transition.

These tensions were present in the development of the early church and still reside within the church today. Carl Dudley and Earle Hilgert in their excellent book, *New Testament Tensions and the Contemporary Church* define "tensions" as "experiences of stress that arise from external and internal problems that stretch the church to the limits of its possibilities, and accompany decisions that challenge the church and may threaten to destroy its effectiveness".[2] They add, "Human social groups tend to follow discernible patterns of development, action and reaction, given analogous circumstances".[3]

The early or primitive church was characterized by five sources of energy; (1) community formation, (2) counterculture, (3) faith crisis and Christian witness, (4) using conflict constructively and (5) rituals of structure and mystery. These streams of ecclesiogenic energy created related tensions; (1)language (identity) vs. vision (ambiguity), (2) intimacy vs. institutionalism, (3)sect vs. society, (4)crisis vs. evangelism and (5) order vs. vitality. These levels of community experience and concomitant tensions are present in every contemporary congregation. The faithful pastor serves by leading the church prayerfully, intentionally and progressively with a passion, purposefulness and plan that resolves these tensions without feuding, fighting or fragmentation.

Every church or community of faith has memory, tradition, and culture. In the nexus of the local church, the biblical story merges quite distinctly with the community's story and the pastor's story. Through its culture, the community or, what we call at First Baptist Church of Chesterfield, "Faith Family," maintains continuity with the past and preserves its distinctiveness in relationship to the larger cultural environment. While this culture or tradition is maintained by symbolic language, acts or ritual, it can also be resistant to change.

Therefore, every congregation has a distinctive DNA! This is my acronym for "Divinely Nurtured Attributes". Understanding the what, how, when, why and where or the genesis and generation of this DNA or unique footprint is an essential function of the pastor as servant leader especially during the formative stages of any new ministry placement and even beyond. As the Greek philosopher Heraclitus noted, "no one steps in the same river twice." Parmenides, a notable critic of Heraclitus responded, "No one steps in the same river once." The inference is that nothing or no one stays the same. Congregational life has more adaptations and versions than Apple! It is imperative that the pastor stays ahead of this shifting curve with current, useful and insightful information.

At the inception of a new pastorate, the pastor must adorn the robe of a cultural diagnostician. It is essential to a successful ministry and easily falls under the caption, "Pastoral Survival and Longevity". Because of eighteen years of prior pastoral experience, when I arrived at First Baptist Church of Chesterfield, Missouri as the newly called pastor on the first Sunday in February 2000, one of my first challenges was to diagnose the culture of the congregation. The historical, psychological and sociological dynamics of the situation were as or more important than its demographics. I was driven by the compulsion to understand the church's culture, corporate personality and history; to gather facts and to create a context for sharing vital information. I became aware in increments during my visits as pastoral candidate and later upon my arrival as pastor-elect that the church was deeply wounded by what had been essentially a civil war between the former pastor and the leadership, particularly the Deacon Ministry. This contention had been divisive, disruptive and too often disagreeable. The scars were deep and had keloid.

In order to facilitate understanding of the culture or environment I had now interfaced and its observable brokenness, I initiated an assessment process called LEAP. LEAP is an acronym for <u>L</u>eadership <u>E</u>valuation <u>A</u>ction <u>P</u>rofile. See Appendix. Over a period of three months, two (2) hour interviews were scheduled and conducted by me with all ministry leaders and other key influencers in the church. These interactions were very productive yielding over time consistent themes, threads and threats that would be used to leverage a long term response that would lead to greater congregational vitality.

In the culture of the local church, comprehension and chronology are conceptually and experientially co-equal and co-eternal. During the <u>LEAP Initiative</u>, no strategic or "second-order" changes were made in the ministry until greater clarity and comprehension of the spiritual and congregational environment was secured. The strategy was exculpatory. Regarding this decision on timing, God spoke to me in a dream that has helpfully haunted me down through the transitional years of this partnership between pastor and people. In the dream there was a long and high wall with scaffolding mounted next to it as far as my eyes could see. While the scaffolding was unattractive, in the dream, the Lord assured me that I must be patient because one day it would be removed and the work on the expansive wall completed. I interpreted this timely revelation as a sign from the Lord to not make hasty decisions at the embryonic stage of my ministry.

It is the reason that I believe the signature hit by country music singer Kenny Rogers should be the theme song of every wise, alert and effective pastor. Rogers says,

> "You've got to know when to hold 'em
> Know when to fold 'em
> Know when to walk away
> And know when to run
> You never count your money

> When you're sittin' at the table
> There'll be time enough for countin'
> When the dealin's done"

The implementation of the LEAP Initiative was reflective of the fact that "the dealins" weren't done. The objective was twofold - understanding the culture and empowering the leaders. During the interviews, key themes, reactions, and perspectives began to emerge. Each leader in turn realized that their ideas, concerns and reactions were valued by the new pastor. Twenty years after this initiative, I still refer to notes taken during these sessions for context during current interactions with some of the same leaders.

In the prior chapter I mentioned my indebtedness to Dr. John Maxwell. In this one, I acknowledge a corresponding debt to Steven Covey and his signature work, *The Seven Habits of Highly Effective People*. Habit # 5 is "Seek First to Understand and Then to Be Understood." Covey says, "If you really seek to understand, without hypocrisy and without guile, there will be times when you will be literally stunned with the pure knowledge and understanding that will flow from another human being".[4] The principle behind this habit undergirded my commitment to LEAP.

I plead guilty to being a history buff with a special affinity for military history. At a church in northern Virginia where I have been graciously and repeatedly invited for conferences and revivals, my host pastor is very much aware of this. He schedules during my visits a tour of one of the historic Civil War battlefields in the area. Our very first exploration was Gettysburg. In this small town in southern Pennsylvania, an epic, bloody struggle occurred between the armies of the Union and the Confederate that significantly impacted the outcome of the war.

The Union's victory had a great deal to do with their securing the high ground during the battle. It allowed the strategic positioning of their forces as the battle ensued and disallowed a Confederate flanking action that could have led to defeat and demoralization of the Union forces. On a hill named Little Round Top, a regiment of soldiers from the state of Maine occupied the high ground and turned back one courageous Confederate assault after another. This was decisive in the battle that took place during July 1 – 3, 1863 and incurred between 46,000 and 51,000 casualties.

A pastor committed to knowing and understanding the community and family of faith he serves is occupying high ground! The Apostle Peter's words to husbands can easily be extrapolated and applied to the relationship between pastor and congregation. He says, ""Likewise, ye husbands, dwell with them according to knowledge, giving honour unto the wife, as unto the weaker vessel, and as being heirs together of the grace of life; that your prayers be not hindered" (1 Pet. 3:7 KJV). We dwell with the people of God, who will one day be the Bride of Christ "according to knowledge." It is the basis of the oft repeated pastoral axiom, "People don't care how much you know until they know how much you care." Engaging the flock of God compassionately, comprehendingly intentionally and experientially is tantamount to Isaiah's "high and lifted up", Ezekiel's "sit where the people sit", and Paul's "caught up in the third heaven" posture, position and perspective that provides viewpoint, validation and victory.

It is critical in any organization for the leader to secure and occupy the high ground. You do not want to fight uphill. It reminds me of a Trustee Ministry workshop I facilitated a few years ago. I shared an illustration of the head of an African tribe whose role as chief required that every day he ascended a high tree and viewed the horizon for potential enemies and threats. A detail of tribesman were stationed at the base of the tree and used their spears to prick, poke and prod the chief whenever required to encourage him to remain at his critical post. Reflective of Acts 6, this pastoral priority provides the precedent for the formation of what would become the office of the deacon in the New Testament. I have been blessed during my pastoral journey by the decorous and dedicated tribesmen of deacons, trustees and other leaders who have stood sentry beneath the high tree of my pastoral calling prompting me to remain providentially positioned at a height where I can scan the horizons for both spiritual foe and spiritual friend.

In those formative years at First Baptist Church of Chesterfield, other assessments were used in the committed trek to "seek first to understand." Christian Swartz's *Natural Church Development* and related survey was definitive and diagnostic in its comprehensiveness, conciseness and clarity. Over the years, periodic assessments have been planned using the excellent tools provided by the Christian Resource Center and the Willow Creek Association. The processional of players and partners in what I describe as pastoral acupuncture includes most recently the Six Styles Leadership Inventory developed by David T. Olson in his book, *Discovering Your Leadership Style – The Power of Chemistry, Strategy and Spirituality*. Olson writes,

> "Your goal as a Christian leader is to help people fulfill God's will for their lives. Rather than achieving this through your own power and position, it is accomplished through drawing on your gifts, personality, passions, habits and character, aided by the work of the Holy Spirit. God's ability to change and transform you into a better leader increases exponentially when you are aware of how other people experience you. Self-awareness increases by being teachable, and teachability is developed through asking incisive questions. You will never be an outstanding leader without understanding these two preconditions.[5]

This assessment has become the basis of our current leadership vetting and validation process that will be used to discover, develop and deploy new servant leaders in the church.

Dedicated and determined surfers enter the water from land with surfboard in tow, then wade out and swim toward and through the oceanic waves thunderously ascending and descending around and over them, bobbling them about like tiny wooden corks in a voluminous and vibrant pool of water. At the right moment, with skillful dexterity and an informed confidence, they mount their boards, stand upright while sustaining their balance as their determined patience is rewarded by the wave that thrillingly transports them to the shore.

Pastors must find and ride the wave created by an intentioned and informed evaluation and diagnosis of congregational culture and history to the solid ground of ministry effectiveness and missional impact.

CHAPTER 9

# BUILDING CARING COMMUNITY

Dr. Martin Luther King, Jr., often spoke of the "beloved community." He published a book of sermons in 1963 titled, *Strength to Love*. In the sermon, "The Man Who Was a Fool," Dr. King said, "In a real sense, all life is interrelated. All men are caught in an inescapable network of mutuality, tied in a single garment of destiny. Whatever affects one directly, affects all indirectly".[1]

Among the prodigious literary offerings of martyred German theologian Dietrich Bonhoeffer were two books that are compelling and complementary - *Cost of Discipleship* and *Life Together*. One book focused on our relationship to God in a vertical plane. The second book addressed our relationship to others in the body of Christ in a horizontal plane.

In the Book of Genesis, Judah, one of the twelve sons of Jacob faced an experiential crisis as he interceded for the life and well-being of his baby brother Benjamin to a then unrecognizable Joseph, whom he and his brothers had betrayed and sold into slavery in Egypt years earlier. He said, "Now therefore when I come to thy servant my father, and the lad *be* not with us; seeing that his life is bound up in the lad's life" (Gen. 44:30 KJV). Bonhoeffer shares a similar concern and compassion when he writes, "The Christian, however, must bear the burden of a brother. He must suffer and endure the brother. It is only when he is a burden that another person is really a brother and not merely an object to be manipulated. The burden of men was so heavy for God Himself that He had to endure the Cross. God verily bore the burden of men in the body of Jesus Christ".[2] Our relationship to God and our relationship to the brother (or sister) are inseparable. Caring is a thread that is inextricably woven and weaved into the garment of Christian community.

Both a vibrant verticality and a healthy horizontality are needed if a pastor and the local church or for that matter, any other Christian entity is to effectively ride the wave of God's purpose, provision and power and move from message to mission, and from vision to victory. Someone or something beyond us must inspire clarity, commitment and cohesiveness in the common endeavor. Motivational virtue directed toward God and functional virtue directed toward others is the titanic tandems and powerful predicates and prerequisites that converge, coalesce, and connect on the vertical and horizontal bar of the Old Rugged Cross.

Like the popular board game Monopoly, pastors are given an initial cache of relational capital. As we move deliberately around the playing board of ministry, we want to build on that initial investiture and expand our relational holdings as priests and ambassadors of Christ. It is this pastoral prospect and possibility that the Apostle Paul assents to when he writes to the church at Corinth these words,

> Do we begin again to commend ourselves? or need we, as some _others_, epistles of commendation to you, or _letters_ of commendation from you? Ye are our epistle written in our hearts, known and read of all men: _Forasmuch as ye are_ manifestly declared to be the epistle of Christ ministered by us,

> written not with ink, but with the Spirit of the
> living God; not in tables of stone, but in fleshy
> tables of the heart" (2 Cor. 3:1-3 KJV).

Ministering to and among God's people is like opening a checking account at a bank. Beyond the initial deposit, additional deposits are made over time so that the checks that are written on the account will clear. Withdrawals are an unavoidable part of ministry. Some withdrawals are substantive and significant and, if there is not enough cash in the account, pastoral checks will bounce! I have dubbed this principle and priority as "relational liquidity". When the Lord Jesus Christ came to this planet, He opened a sizable and significant relational account. Dr. Eugene Peterson's paraphrase of a pivotal text in the Gospel of John characterizes and capsulate this vast and vicarious relational investment.

> "The Word became flesh and blood, and moved
> into the neighborhood. We saw the glory with
> our own eyes, the one-of-a-kind glory, like
> Father, like Son, Generous inside and out,
> true from start to finish" (John 1:14 MSG).

Perfection, while a passionate and prized pursuit, is not a permanent possession. The Psalmist says, "There is none that doeth good" (Ps. 14:1b KJV). In the aforementioned letter to the church at Corinth, the Apostle Paul reminded them and us, "But we have this treasure in earthen vessels, that the excellency of the power may be of God, and not us" (2 Cor. 4:7 KJV). In life and in ministry, our persistent "earthiness" assures that withdrawals will take place in relationships. The late pastor and eminent preacher, Dr. Gardner C. Taylor in his lectures on preaching at the Yale Divinity School used the phrase "humbling negatives".[3] He rightfully posits that we all struggle with something that is withdrawal positive.

Therefore, we minister to, with and among God's people as what Henri Nouwen describes as "wounded healers." In his classic treatise by the same name, *The Wounded Healer*, he shares a Jewish legend from the Talmud where a revered rabbi sits among the poor and disenfranchised covered with wounds. The rabbi unbinds his wounds one at a time and binds them up again saying to himself, "Perhaps I shall be needed." Nouwen makes a compelling application to Christian ministry. He writes,

> "So it is too with the minister. Since it is his task to make visible the first vestiges of liberation for others, he must bind his own wounds carefully in anticipation of the moment when he is needed. He is called to be the wounded healer, the one who must look after his own wounds but at the same time be prepared to heal the wounds of others".[4]

Caring community begins with the ministry of the Consummate Caregiver, "who comforts us in all our troubles, so that we can comfort those in any trouble with the comfort we ourselves have received from God" (2 Cor. 1:4 NIV). The prophet Ezekiel "sat where they (the people) sat" and in the shifting shadow of that existential engagement, God formed and fashioned within him the winged prophecies that gave his people hope in the midst of despair. From this experiential coordinate God summons and subpoenas Ezekiel to answer the question, "Son of man, can these bones live?" (Ezek. 37:3a KJV). Detachment, disinterest or disengagement from the sufferings of the people could have prompted an overconfident, overzealous or prideful response by Ezekiel, but gripped with the magnanimity of the moment and the misery he experienced firsthand, he could only say to God, "O Lord God, thou knowest"(Eze 37:4b KJV).

I am reminded of the story of the little girl whose mother sent her to the neighborhood grocery store to buy some milk. She returned after an inordinately long time and her mother asked, "What took you so long?" The little girl responded, "My friend Sally fell and hurt herself". The mother asked, "What could you do?" The little girl responded, "I sat there with Sally and cried with her."

Pastors must be willing and ready to "Rejoice with them that do rejoice, and weep with them that weep" (Rom 12:15 KJV).

Pastors must prayerfully and actively seek and seize opportunities to build on the initial positional collateral and pastoral capital we receive at the time of the church's call. Otherwise, an ill-fated or unadvised landing on Boardwalk, Park Place (back to the Monopoly metaphor) or some other ministry high rent or high risk district could be calamitous and costly. We do this not because we are calculating but because we are called and because we care. I need look no farther than the mirror to see evidence that the pastoral bread we "cast upon the waters", the relational deposits that we make in the lives of others in crisis, will return to us when needed, and not always from the immediate objects of our labor of love.

The late Dr. Warren Oates's book, *The Christian Pastor* is must reading for every serious pastor. In his book, Oates posits that every Christian pastor comes to his work in the strength of a great heritage. Two thousand years of Christian ministry have conditioned parishioners to expect the presence of their pastors during the crises of life. As "first among equals", the pastor speaks for and to people during the critical moments of the life cycle. According to Oates,

> "Crises are the shared experiences, the straitened anxieties of life that require a

reorganization of personality for individuals and groups, ethical choices, emotional maturity and additional spiritual resources and resolve".[5]

The idea of crisis as it relates to pastoral ministry is rooted in primitive religion's relationship to the periodicity of the life cycle. The Judeo-Christian faith continues to maintain its contact with human life by infusing crisis with religious symbolism and celebration. Whether the dedication of an infant, a funeral service, birthday observance, graduation from school, surgery, wedding, job promotion, unexpected unemployment or relocation, the pastor and local church helps individuals and families maintain personal identity and congruity during times of crisis and transition.

Therefore, the most important asset of the pastor is not personal appeal or charisma nor educational and professional competency but an arresting awareness and appropriate appreciation of the pastoral office within the proper theological context and connection. Contextually, this includes the sovereignty of God, the incarnation of Jesus Christ, the contemporaneity of the Holy Spirit and the function of the church as a spiritual reality in this world. Moreover, an awareness and appreciation of the theological context for pastoral ministry will invest that work with dignity, distinction and durability. To ignore or denigrate the symbolism inherent in the pastoral office, the rich residue of centuries of Christian history and ministry is to commit vocational suicide. The pastor is a representative of God, a symbol of moral righteousness. The pastor is also a representative of Jesus Christ. Through the caring ministry of the faithful pastor, Jesus's life and love receives refreshing and recurring replication.

In the Genesis narrative, God gives Adam the privilege and prerogative to name the creatures that came before him in pairs. God could have told Adam what to call each creature that paraded before him but Adam named them. Early in my ministry at the First Baptist Church of Chesterfield, I exercised my pastoral pedagogical prerogative by coining the phrase "surround care" as a category for congregational care. I shared this concept in more than one setting with key leaders. This metaphor captioned and characterized our love, concern and compassion for the souls God had entrusted in our care. An adaptation of "surround sound", *surround care* was used as a template to enhance the care of existing church members experiencing crisis as well as buttress the healthy and intentional assimilation of those "the Lord daily added to the church". Surrounded by a caring community of which the pastor, deacons and leaders served in the vanguard, the goal was for existing and new members to feel loved, valued and challenged.

Despite a prayerful intentionality in this area, I cannot claim congregational immunity from what Bishop Richard James Neuhaus in his insightful book *Freedom for Ministry* called *ecclesiogenic disease*, the haunting and often hobbling not yet-ness of spiritual community. Neuhaus says,

> "It is especially depressing when the place of healing inflicts new hurts. There is not hate so hateful as the hate that is exercised in the name of Christian love. There is no appeal from it because it is incorporated into itself the point of appeal. The poison has co-opted the antidote".[6]

A few months ago, a new member of our Faith Family shared with me about his tentativeness about getting involved in a ministry. He said, "Pastor, there is no hurt like church hurt". This testimony and a myriad of others remind us that the search for authentic and affective Christian community is illusive. The ground is always shifting and every congregation lives in a perpetual state of "becoming." We are literally tied in "nots". We are not what we used to be, not what we ought to be and not what we are going to be! Both pastor and people share this "not-yetness" and while, congregational life is not always pretty, neither is it petty. The Apostle John writes in his first epistle, "Dear friends, now we are children of God, and what we will be has not yet been made known. But we know that when Christ appears, we shall be like him, for we shall see him as he is. All who have this hope in him purify themselves, just as he is pure" (1 John 3:2-3 NIV).

Pop singer Tina Turner's signature hit, *"What's Love Got to Do With It"* is applicable to the building of caring community in the local church. I find it profoundly moving that in the Upper Room as the sands of the hourglass of time divinely turned and tilted toward the finality and fulfillment of Jesus's earthly ministry, the thirteenth chapter of the Gospel of John erupts with love and ends with love. "Having loved His own who were in the world, He loved them to the end" (John 13:1b NIV). And then in verse 34- 35 He says, "A new command I give you: Love one another. As I have loved you, so you must love one another. By this everyone will know that you are my disciples, if you love one another". Obviously, love has something to do with it!

Noted Christian apologist Dr. Ravi Zacharias argues that worship is the church's greatest evangel. I agree that worshipping God the Father of our Lord and Savior Jesus Christ in the power of the Holy Spirit is a magnet that draws the lost to us. I also believe that, in any attempted ranking, Christian fellowship and a commitment to building caring community, if not first is certainly a close second. It is the beckoning, bold-typed billboard that the world sees when they drive past the church on the busy, bumpy and burdensome highways of life.

During a recent hospital visit while waiting for the nurses to finish attending the patient I had come to see, I walked over to the bulletin board and was intrigued by a collage of cards, letters and notes that the medical staff on that particular floor had received from former patients and their families. Above the flotillas of appreciation and acknowledgments, in large, bold letters were the words, "Why We Do What We Do!" I was so moved by this concrete and compelling affirmation of the priority the doctors, nurses, technicians, housekeeping and other hospital staff had placed on the care of their patients that I returned to the church and immediately launched plans for a similar section on our church bulletin board. That project has been completed, and a recent letter I received from a member reflects the heartbeat of a caring community. It said,

> "Dear Pastor Stubblefield, I wanted to put pen to paper to express sincere appreciation many times over for the blessings, the leadership to teach and preach the Word consistently, to witness with gladness the continued growth of our church in a positive direction; meeting so many challenges. Offering to you, devoted partner Judy, pastoral ministry and all committed participants congratulations on the beautifully organized and successful celebration of the 173rd Church Anniversary ... Pastor, seeing the handsomely poised picture of Phil _in the memorial section of the program_, remembering our beloved initiated immediate tears and smiles... Thanks for all that you do."

This is what happens in a caring community and it is why we do what we do.

CHAPTER 10

# Leading and Leveraging Constructive Cooperation

A servant mindset, cultural intelligence, and caring community are the foundation stones for constructive cooperation in ministry. In the mid-eighties, as a young pastor still cutting his ministry teeth, I attended the Billy Graham School of Evangelism in Washington, D.C. I heard the late Dr. E. V. Hill, then the popular pastor and prolific preacher of the Mt. Zion Missionary Baptist Church in Los Angeles, CA applaud the Billy Graham Evangelistic Association for being "a great team". The School and the unforgettable evangelism crusade I attended were demonstrative of this dynamic.

Andrew Carnegie once said, "Teamwork is the ability to work together toward a common vision. It is the ability to direct individual accomplishment toward organizational objectives. It is the fuel that allows common people to do uncommon work". Hellen Keller said, "Alone we can do so little; together, we can do so much". One of my favorite biblical stories demonstrates these principles.

> And again he entered into Capernaum after *some* days; and it was noised that he was in the house. And straightway many were gathered together, insomuch that there was no room to receive *them*, no, not so much as about the door: and he preached the word unto them. And they come unto him, bringing one sick of the palsy, which was borne of four. And when they could not come nigh unto him for the press, they uncovered the roof where he was: and when they had broken *it* up, they let down the bed wherein the sick of the palsy lay. When Jesus saw their faith, he said unto the sick of the palsy, Son, thy sins be forgiven thee (Mark 2:1-5 KJV)

If I was preaching this text, I would note that it has five movements which delineate the characteristics of an effective team. Would you like to know what they are? I am glad you asked! An effective team (1), has a clear sense of purpose, (2)works together to reach a goal, (3)overcomes obstacles, facing challenges and conflict together, (4)is adaptable and (5)demonstrates a strong faith in the Lord.

In the Old Testament, these characteristics enabled Nehemiah to motivate and mobilize the Jews, who had just returned from exile. Together they were able to rebuild the walls of Jerusalem in only fifty-two days. The Bible records, "So we built the wall; an all the wall was joined together unto the half thereof; for the people had a mind to work (Neh. 4:6 KJV). Evaluating how Nehemiah, the Governor of Judaea leveraged constructive cooperation to rebuild the wall, Cyril Barber in his excellent commentary *Nehemiah and the Dynamics of Effective Leadership* notes, "The first principle of success is seen in the coordination Nehemiah achieved. The clue is found in the recurrence of the phrases, "next to him" or "next to them".[1] If the phrases "after him" and "after them" in the King James Version are added to this analysis, there are twenty-nine occurrences in Chapter 3. This remarkable reiteration and redeeming redundancy reflects something very important and impactful that God wants us to know about His people working together.

In the creation narrative recorded in Chapter One of Genesis, for six consecutive days, God creates all that is by divine command. Over and over again, God says. "Let there be."

But when God prepares to create man, the crown jewel of His creation, He doesn't say "Let there be" but rather, "Let us" (Gen. 1:26 KJV). Man and later, woman would not ultimately be the result of God's sovereign command but rather reflectors of God's sacred community for the God of the Bible is one in essence and three in Person. God the Father, God the Son and God the Holy Spirit <u>cooperated</u> to create the human race. We reflect God's essential essence when we work together to fulfill His divine plan. Fast forward to Calvary, and there on the Cross when Jesus becomes "sin for us", He cries out, "My God, My God, why hast thou forsaken me?" (Mark 15:34 KJV) Just as in creation, in redemption the Son acknowledges the Trinitarian community of which He is One.

Sadly, in the contemporary church, there are more operators than cooperators; more chiefs than Indians or, to use a musical analogy, more soloists than background singers. Oneness, unity, cooperation, and shared purpose are exceptions and not the rule. Many churches are mired in mediocrity, crippled by the commonplace, obsessed with the ordinary and hostage to the habitual because of the inability to work "next to him" or "next to her". The "us versus them" mentality has gone viral and, if not abated, will reach pandemic proportions. Kennon L. Callahan in his book, *Twelve Keys to an Effective Church*, writes,

> "People are not simply searching for contracts; they are searching for covenant. They are not searching for programs and activities

or institutional structures, but for proleptic experiences of kingdom and events of mission in which they can share. They are not searching for a merry-go-round of business activities and committee meetings; they are searching for people with whom they can live out <u>*life together*</u> *[emphasis mine]*".[2]

Life together is the ideal that we dare not cease or desist from pursuing however illusive it might be. The stakes are much too high! Jesus said, "And if a kingdom be divided against itself; that kingdom cannot stand" (Mark 3:24 KJV). The pastor who is serious about riding the wave of a unique calling and fulfilling the vision and mission of the church he serves will lead and leverage constructive cooperation by precept and example.

CHAPTER 11

# CREATING FUNCTIONAL STRUCTURES

A few years ago, while attending the E. K. Bailey Expository Preaching Conference in Dallas, Texas, I listened to Dr. Joel Gregory, currently Professor of Preaching at Baylor University, author and former Pastor of the First Baptist Church of Dallas, Texas as he shared a compelling sermon illustration. According to Gregory, Dr. George W. Truett, one of his predecessors at First Baptist Church of Dallas and a giant in the Southern Baptist Convention, was preaching a revival at a small church outside of Dallas. On this particular evening, he was especially disappointed with his sermonic presentation. During the drive back, he asked one of his faithful deacons who had chauffeured him to the service, what he thought about the message that evening. Dr. Truett respected this deacon for his candor and insight. The deacon responded, "Doc, I believe you tried to build a cathedral on a chicken coop foundation."

My earliest interaction and experiences as pastor with the leadership and members of the First Baptist Church of Chesterfield focused on creating a ministry infrastructure that was both faithful to the principles of the Word of God and functional. I remember a pivotal meeting with the Deacons early in my tenure when I told them, "We owe this church a strong Pastor and Deacon Ministry. Because of challenges and conflict, other pastors and churches have adopted other models, but for us there would be no alternative paths." Exodus 18, Acts 6, Philippians 1 and 1 Timothy 3 would be our templates.

My resolve regarding this non-negotiable paradigm and priority was reminiscent of the decision of the young and brilliant military strategist and leader of men, Alexander the Great who, when his army landed in Persia ordered the ships that brought them there burned. He was confronted by his generals for what they perceived was a reckless act. They asked him, "How are we going to get home?" Alexander responded, "By defeating the Persians." In order to return home, using the title of a recent sermon I preached, they would have to "go all out for the all in!" The Deacons and I would face the Persians together.

This was and remains a key component in the infrastructure that undergirds the ministry of the church. Others were added as well. As I accumulated pastoral capital and credibility, in order to encourage unity, enhance communication and create synergy, Deacons and Trustees, the spiritual and fiduciary leadership of the church were united in what is called the "Joint Ministry." The predicate and precedent was established early in the ministry major decisions or initiatives would launch from this leadership precipice. This was our spiritual Cape Canaveral.

I organized the Primary Initiative Vision Optimization Team (PIVOT), consisting of the Pastor, Chairmen of the Deacon and Trustee Ministry, Chairman of the Joint Ministry and Church Treasurer. This small group of core leaders functioned as an echo chamber, quick response, and quick strike unit for me as the Holy Spirit moved me from message to specific and strategic initiatives that would advance the mission of the church. The PIVOT would become the predecessor of our current Executive Ministry Team (EMT).

The Office of the Pastor, Executive Ministry Team, and Joint Ministry are the cornerstones of our current ministry infrastructure. Individual ministries are organized around a Pillar structure where ministers, deacons and trustee provide oversight and guidance. See Addendum.

In ministry, it takes three things to make the right thing. Proper content produces proper character, and proper character produces proper consequences. Consequently, a crucial component of the "functional structures" that we were creating at the First Baptist Church of Chesterfield was a "content intensive" focus on Christian education. Sunday school, Bible study and Evangelism Training would be the flagships of our Christian armada and provide the spiritual armaments and ornaments that would undergird the work of ministry. Accountability standards were put in place for leaders who were required to be involved in one or all of these Christian education components. See the Servant-Leader Covenant in the Addendum.

How significant is this? Dr. Charles Simeon (1759 -1836), a noted Anglican pastor is considered by many scholars as the father of expository preaching. It is reported that a young pastor came to him once seeking his wise and tenured counsel regarding some challenges he was having at the church he served. The young minister was so frustrated that he was considering resigning and moving on to greener pastures. He shared with Dr. Simeon some of the dynamics of the situation he was experiencing.

Simeon, responded with a story about two ships that had run aground. Impatient, the captain of one ship decided to hire a team of horses to pull the ship back into the waters. The ship was torn apart by the force of this ill-advised extraction. The other captain, much more patient said, "I will wait until the tide rises and the waves will take the ship back into the sea." Simeon said to the young preacher and pastor, "When the tide rise, everything in the harbor floats out to sea." Simeon was emphasizing the primacy of the Word of God in the life of the church and the ministry of the pastor. This illustration has helpfully haunted me as a pastor because an effective, biblically grounded Christian education ministry has "tide-rising" potential. Preach and teach the word authentically, consistently and demonstrably and the drift wood and debris that suffocate ministry will float out to sea.

Because a picture is worth a thousand words, when creating functional structures, I do want to emphasize the importance of imaging and concretizing the message and mission of the church. In my second year as pastor and every year since, after a season of prayer and reflection I recommend to the leadership and the church some inundation of the theme "Awakening to Our Potential - Going Further Out and Deeper Down." This theme is adopted at our annual congregational meeting. In 2020, the focus will be on "Staying the Course." Leadership training and orientation, event planning and messaging are built around this annual theme. During the first two months of each calendar year, the pastor preaches a sermon series that amplifies and galvanizes this theme in the hearts and minds of the people. See Addendum.

In Habakkuk 2:2, the prophet writes "And the LORD answered me, and said, Write the vision, and make it plain upon the tables, that he may run that readeth it" (KJV). This biblical principle is consensual and complimentary of the impact of a conceptual image. Compelling images and thematic threads are critical contributors to the functionality of any ministry. Positive and inclusive change that encourages more participation is like "a sponge that creates the capacity for enhanced spiritual absorbency". God calls the church to be "a thermostat that controls and impacts its environment and not just a thermometer that records the temperature". First Baptist Church of Chesterfield is "not a destination but a hub". Because of the transitional nature of our ministry we are "equipping disciples for Christian service" who will serve other congregations.

I have already mentioned "surround care" in a previous chapter. When faced with a difficult decision, leaders are encouraged to "err on the side of love" and "not to set a precedent we can't live with." First Baptist Church of Chesterfield is "a local church with a global mission", our Thanksgiving outreach initiative, "Touches of Love Delivered" (TOLD), and "ramp up" (the planning and preparation process for congregational meetings) are all images and themes that are embedded in the culture of the church.

Functionality is encouraged and enhanced by the intentional and prayerful creation of a secondary; even subliminal language that saturates and seasons the culture. This is not a case of "one size fits all" but every pastor must seek God's guidance while creating functional organizational and conceptual structures that enable and energize the work of ministry.

CHAPTER 12

# Practicing Self Care

My grandfather's farm in rural West Tennessee was always bustling with activity. I can remember as a child being fascinated with all the livestock; cows, pigs, mules, and chickens or riding on the back of the tractor with him as if I was enjoying one of the major attractions at the Disney World Theme Park in Orlando, Florida. I remember hoeing and picking cotton from sun up to sun down or watching him, my grandmother, mother, aunts and older cousin mesh and merge the sorghum stalks we grew through a press to make molasses for family consumption and for the local market.

One of my most vivid memories that still helpfully haunts me is the water well outside the small four room frame house that was our home. Fresh water for cooking and cleaning was supplied by a stream that emptied into the pool beneath the ground where the well stood. Water was retrieved with a long circular bucket attached to a rope which was let down in the well. When dining at a Cracker Barrel, I grow nostalgic when I see one of those buckets displayed as an artifact on the wall of the restaurant.

Drawing water was one of my assigned chores. It was a matter of common knowledge that after the third bucket was filled, lifted with the rope from the pool beneath the ground and emptied, time had to be allowed for the water in the pool below to replenish itself otherwise that fourth bucket would be brownish, muddy and not suitable for drinking. Whenever I read Jesus's words to the woman of Samaria in John, Chapter 4, I think of this limitation. Jesus said to her, ""But whosoever drinketh of the water that I shall give him shall never thirst; but the water that I shall give him shall be in him a well of water springing up into everlasting life" (John 4:14 KJV). Our little well did not have the power or capacity of unlimited replenishment. Neither do any of us!

It has been said more than once that "hindsight is 20/20". If I could seize an opportunity for a "do over" after almost forty years of pastoral ministry, I would exercise greater intentionality around implementing what Dr. Bill Hybels tagged at a conference I attended a few years ago as "replenishment strategies". At this conference and others that followed, I started hearing presenters and facilitators talk about "self-care", "replenishment" and "sharpening exercises". Maybe these concepts and strategies were being articulated before but I wasn't listening.

There is ecstasy and agony in Christian ministry especially the pastorate. I often say that "ministry is a splendid misery." That is why the "call" is essential and non-negotiable. No one adorns the pastoral mantle without Divine unction. The ecstatic, unforgettable highs on Mount Hermon where we like the Apostle Peter, say, "It is good to be here" (Mk 9:5 KJV) are followed closely by the discouraging descents into the valley of suffering where we are met with the caretakers of the dark, the desperate and the demonic who taunts, teases and terrorizes us with the indictment, "and I spake to thy disciples that they should cast him out; and they could not" (Mark 9:18 KJV).

Ministry is demanding, draining and stressful. Even the Master was not exempt. When the woman with the issue of blood touched the hem of his garment, the Bible says, ""And Jesus, immediately knowing in himself that virtue had gone out of him, turned him about in the press, and said, Who touched my clothes?" (Mark 5:30 KJV). In his excellent book, *Contemporary Insights from Bible Characters*, Paul Culbertson comments on the meltdown and letdown that the prophet Elijah experience after his victory at Mount Carmel recorded in 1 Kings, Chapter 18, he writes,

> "It seems obvious that Elijah was physically and psychologically exhausted. He had urged King Ahab to eat and drink (1 Kings 18:41) but probably failed to do so himself. Rest and sleep had been out of the question. There was too much excitement! And it was no small task to liquidate the 450 false prophets in an all-day confrontation. Then his 17 mile, cross-country run ahead of Ahab's royal chariot drained all of his reserve supply of energy".
>
> Now sitting alone with both his physical and psychic energy at an all-time low, his problems were seen as completely insoluble and overwhelming. His response was, "It is enough; now, O Lord, take away my life; for I am not better than my fathers" (1 Kings 19:4 KJV).[1]

Ten years ago in my hometown of Paris, Tennessee, I facilitated a session at a pastor's conference. I tagged my session, *Ministry Burnout - Coming Apart or Come Apart - The Unhurried Life*. I asked the pastors present, "Why is pastoral ministry so stressful?" After a sustained, serious and substantive interaction around subject matter that truly mattered to all of us, I shared the following reasons.

- Disparity between expectations and reality
- Lack of clearly defined boundaries
- Conflicted identity - being a leader and servant at the same time

- Ambiguity; intangibility - how do I know I'm making a difference?
- Measuring effectiveness
- Confusing role with image - deriving too much self-esteem from what we do
- Time management challenges
- Multiplicity of roles
- Conflicted environment
- Challenge of balancing structure and spontaneity
- Administrative overload
- Lack of core friendships

Pastor Kirk Byron Jones in a candidly transparent confrontation of this issue in his book, *Rest in the Storm – Self-Care Strategies for Clergy and Other Caregivers* while facing his own burnout crisis was moved by the account of Jesus calming the stormy sea in Mark 4:35-41. He writes,

> "Over the years I have come to understand Mark's passage as not only a literary source of relief, but also a living model for learning how to cope with conditions of overload and overdrive. Jesus's actions on the boat that night can guide us out of our storms and stress, and keep us from needlessly riding into such storms in the first place. I am convinced that both what happened and what did _not_ happen on the boat that night offer critical insights into resisting overload and overdrive in everyday living. If we can understand and practice the behaviors Jesus exhibited on the boat, we can experience peace amid the storms of life-threatening stress".[2]

The late Dr. Eugene Peterson remains my spiritual mentor. In his classic commentary on pastoral ministry, *The Contemplative Pastor*, he offers a striking metaphor. Peterson insists that there are two perils to ministry - "flurry and hurry". With typical candor and clarity he writes, "Flurry dissipates ministry and hurry constipates it." Citing Herman Melville's classic novel, Moby Dick, Peterson insightfully observes,

> "There is a turbulent scene in which a whaleboat scuds across a frothing ocean in pursuit of the great white, Moby Dick. The sailors are laboring fiercely, every muscle taunt, all attention and energy concentrated on the task. The cosmic conflict between good and evil is joined; chaotic sea and demonic sea monster versus the morally outraged man, Captain Ahab. In this boat however, there is one man who does nothing. He doesn't hold an oar; he doesn't perspire; he doesn't shout. He is languid in the crash and the cursing. This man is the harpooner, quiet and poised, waiting." And then Peterson writes this sentence that forever remains etched in my consciousness, "To insure the greatest efficiency in the dart, the harpooners of this world must start to their feet out of idleness, and not out of toil".[3]

The Christian pastor is a "poised harpooner". But burnout and stress destroys our competence, capacity and courage to "throw the dart." The problem is that we are TOO BUSY!!!! A million distractions keep us from experiencing on a regular basis what Dr. John Ortberg describes as the "unhurried life." Hurry sickness is disease that is unique to our contemporary culture. The plethora of choices are endless and so often our inability to control this area of our lives rob us of the opportunity to have a more intimate relationship with God and with others. Depleted, we become what Bishop Fulton Sheen, Catholic priest and radio personality characterized as "empty perfume bottles."

As you ride the wave of your own pastoral calling, I am sharing this final summons with you just nine months removed from a ministry sabbatical. With the support of our leadership and the encouragement of the members of our Faith Family, I withdrew from my pastoral labor of love for two months. No preaching, teaching, hospital visits, administration, conflict management or counseling. Just rest and precious time to renew mind, spirit and body. I regret that I didn't do this much sooner.

As we practice self-care, we must recover the Sabbath Principle recorded in Genesis Chapter 1. The theological basis of the Sabbath rests in God's activity in creation. The Bible begins with God engaged in the activity of creation. For six days, God creates all that is. It is important to note that the Hebrew day began with evening. Morning was the culmination of God's creative work on each day of creation. Repeatedly in the narrative we encounter the phrase, "And the evening and the morning ..." See Gen. 1:5; 8; 13; 19; 23; 31. Again, Eugene Peterson shares wonderful insight into the significance of this pattern. He writes,

> "The Hebrew evening/morning sequence conditions us to the rhythms of grace. We go to sleep, and God begins his work. As we sleep he develops his covenant. We wake and are called out to participate in God's creative action. We respond in faith, in work. But always grace is previous. Grace is primary. We wake into a world we didn't make, into a salvation we didn't earn. Evening: God begins, without our help, his creative day. Morning: God calls us to enjoy and share and develop the work he initiated. Creation and covenant are sheer grace and there to greet us every morning".[4]

The Psalmist captured and capsulated this theme when he wrote, " "It is a good thing to give thanks unto the Lord, and to sing praises unto thy name, O most High: To shew forth thy lovingkindness in the morning, and thy faithfulness every night," (Ps. 92:1-2 KJV). Dr. Lelan Ryken in his book *Redeeming the Time: A Christian Approach to Work and Leisure* says the same thing in a different way. He writes, "Earlier in this century someone claimed that we work at our play and play at our work. Today the confusion has deepened: we worship our work, work at our play, and play in our worship".[5] Pastors if we are not prayerful and purposeful regarding matters of self-care" and "replenishment" we become the biggest perpetuators of this fraud and fallacy. What color is the water in your bucket?

> "It is well to live in the valley sweet,
> Where the work of the world is done,
> Where the reapers sing in the fields of wheat,
> As they toil till the set of sun.
> But beyond the meadows, the hills I see
> Where the noises of traffic cease,
> And I follow a Voice that calleth to me
> From the hilltop regions of peace.
> Aye, to live is sweet in the valley fair,
> And to toil till the set of sun;
> But my spirit yearns for the hilltop's air
> When the day and its work are done.
> For a Presence breathes o'er the silent hills,
> And its sweetness is living yet;
> The same deep calm all the hillside fills,
> As breathed over Olivet."
>
> From *Streams in the Desert* by L. B. E. Cowman

# Endnotes

## Chapter 1

[1] Aubrey Malphurs, *Developing a Vision for Ministry in the 21st Century* (Grand Rapids: Baker Books, 1999), p. 85.

[2] James W. Cox, *Preaching* (San Francisco: Harper and Row Publishers, 1985), p. 45.

[3] Howard Thurman, *Deep River and the Negro Spiritual Speaks of Life and Death* (Richmond, Indiana: Friends Press, 1975), p. 11.

[4] William H. Myers, "The Hermeneutical Dilemma of the African American Biblical Student" in *Stony the Road We Trod – African American Biblical Interpretation*, ed. Cain Hope Felder (Minneapolis: Fortress Press), pp. 44-50.

[5] Thurman, p. 36.

[6] James R. Nieman, "Preaching that Drives People from Church," *Currents in Theology and Missions*, 20 (April 1993), pp. 106-115.

## Chapter 2

[1] Samuel Volbeda, *The Pastoral Genius of Preaching* (Grand Rapids: Zondervan, 1960), p. 68.

[2] John R. W. Stott, *Between Two World - The Art of Preaching in the Twentieth Century* (Grand Rapids: Eerdmans, 1982) p. 135.

[3]James M. Gordon, *Evangelical Spirituality - from the Wesleys to John Stott* (London: SPCK, 1991), p. 5.

[4]Richard George Eli, "The Prophetic Ministry of the Pastor", *Asia Journal of Theology* 1(October 1987), p. 375.

[5]Cox, p. 32.

[6]Thurman, pp. 11-12.

[7]Miles Jones, "Preaching Papers," *Hampton and Virginia Union Lectures*, (Martin Luther King Fellows Press, 1998), pp. 38-39.

[8]Dallas Willard, *The Spirit of the Disciplines - Understanding How God Changes Lives* (San Francisco: Harper, 1991), p. 15.

[9]Robert Stackel, "Pastoral Preaching", *Lutheran Quarterly*, 20 (November 1968), p. 367.

# Chapter 3

[1]George Barna, *Leading Your Church Forward* (Ventura, CA: Barna Research Group, Ltd, 2003), pp. 8-9.

[2]Stott, p. 57.

[3]Ravi Zacharias, *Can Man Live Without God* (Dallas: Word Publishing, 1994), pp. 85-91.

[4]Stott, p. 58.

[5]C. Stephen Evans, *Why We Believe? Reason and Mystery As Pointers to God* (Grand Rapids: Eerdmans, 1996), p. 31.

[6]Ibid., pp. 58-60.

[7]Walter Brueggemann, "Preaching as Imagination," *Theology Today*, 52 (October 1995), p. 321.

## Chapter 4

1 Thomas Rainer, *Eating the Elephant – Bite Sized Steps to Achieve Long-Term Growth in Your Church* (Nashville: Broadman, 1994) p. 19.

## Chapter 5

[1] George Peters, *A Biblical Theology of Missions* (Chicago: Moody Press, 1972), p. 65.

[2] Ibid., p. 81.

[3] W. O. Carver, *Mission in the Plan of the Ages* (Nashville: Broadman, 1951), p. 12.

[4] Wright, "The Old Testament and Christian Mission," in *Evangel* (Summer 1996), p. 38.

[5] Donald Senior and Carol Stuhmueller, *The Biblical Foundations for Missions* (New York: Orbison's, 1984), pp. 151-156.

[6] Phillips Brooks, *Lectures on Preaching* (Grand Rapids: Baker Book House. Original Printing New York: E. P. Dutton & Company, 1907), p. 5.

[7] George B. Rogers, "The Foolishness of Preaching," in *Interpretation*, 45 (July 1991), pp. 245.

[8] Gardner C. Taylor, *How Shall They Preach* (Elgin, Illinois: Progressive Baptist Publishing House, 1977), p. 29.

[9] Dallas Willard, *The Spirit of the Disciplines - Understanding How God Changes Lives* (San Francisco: Harper, 1991), p. 52.

[10] Gordon, p. 2.

[11] Desales, *Introduction to the Devout Life*, translated by John K. Ryan (New York: Image Books, 1989), p. 35.

[12] Willard, p. 42.

[13] Andrew Murray, *Humility - The Beauty of Holiness* (Fort Washington, Pa: Christian Literature Crusade, 1995), p. 75.

[14] Ibid., p. 76.

[15] Desales, p. 40.

[16] Brother Lawrence, *The Practice of the Presence of God*, Translated by John J. Delaney (New York: Image Books, 1977), p. 51.

[17] Henry H. Mitchell, *Black Preaching - The Recovery of a Powerful Art* (San Francisco: Harper and Row, 1979), p. 106.

[18] Lawrence, p.69.

[19] Lawrence, p. 56.

[20] George A. Lane, *Christian Spirituality - A Historical Sketch* (Chicago: Loyola University Press, 1984), pp. 15-31.

# Chapter 6

[1] Leith Anderson, *Dying for a Change* (Minneapolis: Bethany House, 1990), p. 136.

[2] Ibid., pp. 188-191.

[3] C. S. Lewis, *Mere Christianity*, (San Francisco: Harper Collins, 2001) p. 71.

[4] Robert Dale, *Pastoral Leadership* (Nashville: Abington Press, 1986), pp. 28-32.

[5] Doug Murren, "The Leader as Change Agent", *Leaders on Leadership*, ed. George Barna (Ventura: Regal, 1997) p. 205.

[6] Dale, pp. 88-92.

[7] Manuel L. Scott, *From a Black Brother* (Nashville: Broadman Press, 1971), p. 14.

## Chapter 7

[1] John Maxwell, *Twenty One Irrefutable Laws of Leadership* (Nashville: Thomas Nelson, 1998), pp. 5-6.

[2] Earnest O. White, *Becoming a Christian Leader* (Nashville: Convention Press, 1985), p. 24.

[3] Dale, p. 29.

## Chapter 8

[1] Charles H. Kraft, *Christianity in Culture* (New York: Orbis Books, 1990), p. 47.

[2] Carl S. Dudley and Earle Hilgert, *New Testament Tensions and the Contemporary Church* (Philadelphia: Fortress Press, 1987), p. 1.

[3] Ibid., p. 5.

[4] Stephen R. Covey, *The 7 Habits of Highly Effective People*, (New York: Simon & Schuster, 1989), p. 252.

[5] David T. Olson, *Discovering Your Leadership style – The Power of Chemistry, Strategy and Spirituality* (Downers Grove, IL: IVP Books), p. 30.

## Chapter 9

[1] Martin Luther King, Jr., *Strength to Love* (Philadelphia: Fortress Press, 1963), p. 70.

[2] Dietrich Bonhoeffer, *Life Together*, (New York: Harper and Row Publishers, 1954.

[3] Taylor, p. 70.

[4] Henri Nouwen, *The Wounded Healer* (Garden City, New York: Image Books, 1979) p. 82.

[5] Wayne Oates, *The Christian Pastor* (Philadelphia: The Westminster Press, 1982) p. 18.

[6] Richard John Neuhaus, *Freedom for Ministry* (Grand Rapids: Eerdmans Publishing Company, 1979), p. 123.

## Chapter 10

[1] Cyril J. Barber, *Nehemiah and the Dynamics of Effective Leadership* (Neptune: Loizeaux Brothers, 1978) p. 49.

[2] Kennon L. Callahan, *Twelve Keys to an Effective Church* (San Francisco: Harper and Row, 1983), p. 35.

## Chapter 12

[1] Paul T. Culbertson, *Contemporary Insights from Bible Characters*, (Grand Rapids: Baker Book House, 2014), p. 13.

[2] Kirk Byron Jones, *Rest in the Storm – Self-Care Strategies for Clergy and Other Caregivers* (Valley Forge: Judson Press, 2001), p. 24.

[3] Eugene Peterson, *The Contemplative Pastor* (Grand Rapids: William B. Eerdmans Publishing Company, 1989), pp. 24-25.

[4] Eugene Peterson, *Working the Angles – The Shape of Pastoral Integrity* (Grand Rapids: William B. Eerdmans Publishing Company, 1987), pp. 68-69.

[5] Lelan Ryken, *Redeeming the Time: A Christian Approach to Work and Leisure* (Grand Rapids: Baker Book House, 1995).

# Addendum

## LEADERSHIP EVALUATION ACTION PROFILE (LEAP)

### INTERVIEW GRID

| | |
|---|---|
| **PARTICIPANT** | NAME OF MINISTRY LEADER OR STAFF |
| **PURPOSE** | MINISTRY ASSESSMENT |
| **FOCUS AREAS** | SPIRITUAL PILGRIMMAGE |
| | MINISTRY DYNAMICS<br>   MEMBERS<br>   (ACTIVE/INACTIVE) |
| | MEETING TIMES |
| | ROLE OF MINISTRY AT FBCC |
| | CONCERNS/SUPPORT ISSUES |
| | EQUIPPING NEEDS –<br>   WHAT RESOURCES DO YOU<br>   NEED IN ORDER TO BECOME<br>   A BETTER LEADER? |
| | TEAM LEADERSHIP<br>   IMPLEMENTATION<br>   RECOMMENDATIONS<br>   EXPECTATIONS<br>   FOLLOW-UP |

# THE 7 PILLARS OF DISCIPLESHIP

**EMPOWER · ENABLE · EVANGELIZE · EXALT · EQUIP · ENGAGE · ENHANCE**

**EQUIPPING SOULS FOR CHRISTIAN SERVICE**

**THE WORD OF GOD**

First Baptist Church of Chesterfield
*Equipping Souls for Christian Service*

First Baptist Church of Chesterfield
17103 Wild Horse Creek Road
Chesterfield, MO 63005
636-537-8748 (Phone) / 636-537-4873 (Fax)
www.firstbcc.org

Dr. T.D. Stubblefield, Pastor-Teacher

## OBJECTIVE

To render unto the Lord the adoration He deserves by efficiently aligning the resources and gifts He has given our Faith Family. The pillars are designed to ensure the projects and programs of all ministries, committees and teams emulate the mission and vision of FBCC as manifested through our collective service and worship to our Lord and Savior, Jesus Christ.

## 7 PILLAR TEAMS

Each pillar has been assigned lead Ministers, Deacons and Trustees who are teamed to share oversight and administration. If a ministry has a need, their first point of contact is with the pillar lead that provides direction for that specified area:

> Minister (Office of the Pastor liaison)
> Deacon (Spiritual Content/Insight)
> Trustee (Fiduciary/Operations)

> "Moses' father-in-law replied, "What you are doing is not good. You and these people who come to you will only wear yourselves out. The work is too heavy for you; you cannot handle it alone. Moses listened to his father-in-law and did everything he said. He chose capable men from all Israel and made them leaders of the people, officials over thousands, hundreds, fifties and tens. They served as judges for the people at all times. The difficult cases they brought to Moses, but the simple ones they decided themselves."
> Exodus 18:17—18; 24—26 (NIV)

## EXALT
## (Worship)

The EXALT Pillar is the centralized place where all worship ultimately flows. We endeavor to meet the emerging needs of FBCC through offering excellence in hospitality, praise and worship. Our charge is to honor and esteem God at every juncture in ministry. We magnify and give thanks to the Father without reservation as we worship Him in spirit and in truth.

> "Glorify the LORD with me; let
> us exalt his name together."
> Psalm 34:3 (NIV)

## EMPOWER
## (Congregational Care)

The EMPOWER Pillar's ministries help position the church for long-term stability, long-term maturity and long-term growth. We accomplish this goal by building the "Family Unit" through strong marriages and healthy relationships. The family is God's creation. It is the most essential and most noble of all human institutions. When families are healthy and functional, the sacred society of God forever prospers.

> "I have given you authority to trample on snakes
> and scorpions and to overcome all the power of
> the enemy; nothing will harm you. However,
> do not rejoice that the spirits submit to you, but
> rejoice that your names are written in heaven."
> Luke 10:19—20 (NIV)

## ENABLE
### (Committees)

The ENABLE Pillar consists of committees that support the body of Christ through work that encompasses the continued advancement of Kingdom building as FBCC strives to achieve our vision of being a local church, with a global mission.

> "For we are his workmanship, created in Christ Jesus for good works, which God prepared beforehand, that we should walk in them."
> Ephesians 2:10 (NIV)

## EVANGELIZE
### (Outreach)

The EVANGELIZE Pillar is comprised of ministry movement that has the mission of reaching those outside the walls of our sanctuary with the message, hope and love of Jesus Christ. We do this by ministering to all that we meet, understanding that we are blessed to be a blessing.

> "Every good and perfect gift is from above, coming down from the Father of the Heavenly lights, who does not change like shifting shadows."
> James 1:17 (NIV)

## EQUIP
### (Christian Education)

The EQUIP Pillar is the foundation of the Christian educational arm of FBCC. Its ministries equip the members for ministry and service unto God and God's people through the execution of teaching and training believers to spread the gospel of Jesus Christ, while living lives that exemplify our faith in Him.

> "All Scripture is God—breathed and is useful for teaching, rebuking, correcting and training in righteousness, so that the servant of God may be thoroughly equipped for every good work."
> 2 Timothy 3:17—18 (NIV)

## ENGAGE
### (Mass Communications)

The ENGAGE Pillar consists of ministries/teams responsible for creatively getting members involved in Christian service and engaged in ministry activities through visual and digital communications.

> "Then the Lord replied: "Write down the revelation and make it plain on tablets so that a herald may run with it."
> Habakkuk 2:2 (NIV)

## ENHANCE
### (Physical Property Upkeep/Facility Usage)

The ENHANCE Pillar houses ministries/teams whose focus is the maintenance, upkeep, beautification and usage of God's property, as well as ensuring the premises are secured at all times.

> "The earth is the Lord's, and everything in it, the world, and all who live in it; for he founded it on the seas and established it on the waters."
> Psalm 24:1—2 (NIV)

# SERVANT LEADER COVENANT

Merciful and Loving Lord, we come today to renew our commitment to you and to those who have entrusted us with the servant ministry of leadership. Regardless of any boasts to the contrary, we know that you are the Supreme and Sole source of our strength and joy. Today, we acknowledge our sincere desire to lead by precept and example; to grow in the grace and the knowledge of the Lord Jesus Christ by being steadfast in prayer and diligent in the study of the Word of God in Sunday School, Bible Study and Evangelism and Discipleship Training. As we faithfully execute our sacred responsibilities in this church, we pledge our commitment to be good stewards of your time, talent, tithe, treasure and temple for we are not our own but have been bought with a price, the precious blood of the Lord Jesus Christ. Therefore, we desire to honor the Lord our God with our bodies, mind and spirit which belong to you. We commit as well to working together and bearing one another's burdens knowing that you have commanded us to "love one another for by this all men will know that we are your disciples." We thank you O God for the opportunity to serve You and these your people as together, we renew our commitment to equipping souls for Christian service.
AMEN

# 2019 ANNUAL CHURCH THEME

"Awakening to our Potential
Going Further Out and Deeper Down
Being the Church, Changing the World"

*SERMON SERIES SUMMARY*
*THE CHURCH THAT CHANGES THE WORLD IS ...*

**Part 1 - Christ Redeemed**
Sermon - *The Reliable Redeemer* (Job 19:25-27)

**Part 2 - Spirit Directed**
Sermon - *The Promised Provision* (Luke 16:5-11)

**Part 3 - Bible Believing**
Sermon - *The Timeless Truth* (Acts 17:10-12)

**Part 4 - Pastor Led**
Sermon - *The Compassionate Communicator* (Jeremiah 3:15; Ephesians 4:11)

**Part 5 - Leadership Supported**
Sermon - *The Compelling Constant* (1 Chronicles 12:32; 2 Timothy 2:1-2)

**Part 6 - Congregation Serving**
Sermon - *The Productive Partnership* (Nehemiah 4:6)

**Part 7 - World Changing**
Sermon - *The Mission Mandate* (Psalm 67)

# ROUNDTABLE QUESTIONS & DISCUSSION STARTERS

## Chapter 1
### Introduction

The author compares the gift of pastor-teacher to an "oceanic wave". What do you think about this analogy?

The author says, "The church is not a 'one trick pony'". This is especially true in his faith tradition. What do you think he means and what is the relevance for pastoral preaching and leadership?

What hermeneutical challenge does the Black preacher-pastor share with clerics from other oppressed minorities?

## Chapter 2
### Preaching and the Biblical and Theological Foundations of the Church's Mission

How does the pastor-teacher equip the local church for ministry? What is required for the pastor's ministry to create "spiritual cohesiveness?"

What do you think of the author's dual description of the pastoral function as "leading and feeding"?

How is the ministry of the pastor and pastoral preaching incarnational?

## Chapter 3
### The Revelatory Constellation of Preaching

What is the primary assumption at the heart of pastoral preaching?

Why and how is Christianity a relationship and not a religion?

The author believes that pastoral preaching takes place at the intersection where the truth about God meets the truth about us. What do you think?

## Chapter 4
## The Preacher and Mission Holism – Part 1

What were the two challenges that the author faced as the newly-called pastor of the First Baptist Church of Chesterfield, Missouri? How does this compare to your experience?

What is the foundation on which any local church's mission stands?

## Chapter 5
## The Preacher and Mission Holism – Part 2

What does it mean to describe God as "outgoing and missionary"?

How does the pastor's personality and spirituality advance or impede the work of ministry?

Discuss *ethos, pathos and logos*, the classic divisions of ancient rhetoric and their relationship to the mission of the pastor-teacher.

## Chapter 6
## The Preacher as Change Agent

How does the credibility of the biblical messenger and the biblical message impact change and transition in the local church?

The author argues that effective pastoral work involves "sociological awareness" of the congregation. What do you think about this concept?

## Chapter 7
## The Greatest Among You

What does it mean to be a servant leader? Are the words "servant" and "leader" antithetical or complementary?

What does Jesus teach us about servanthood? How did He demonstrate this model?

## Chapter 8
## Diagnosing and Engaging the Culture

The author believes every local church or congregation has a distinctive DNA or footprint. What does this mean?

In a new pastorate, when and how is a pastor a "cultural diagnostician"?

What is pastoral "high ground" and how do you get there?

## Chapter 9
## Building a Caring Community

Explain the comparison between "relational capital" and the Monopoly board game in the pastor's ministry.

How is the pastor a "wounded healer"?

What does the word "crisis" mean in the ministry of the pastor and the life of the local church?

## Chapter 10
## Leading and Leveraging Constructive Cooperation

What are the five (5) characteristics of an effective team based on Mark 2:1-5? Discuss.

God is a community of "Three". What are the implications of this Trinitarian truth for Christian ministry?

**Chapter 11**
**Creating Effective Structures**

Is "infrastructure" something the church has or is it relegated to the corporate world?

What ministry in the local church has "tide-raising" capability and why?

Conceptual and graphic (pictorial) images are important as the pastor leads the local church from message to mission. Why?

**Chapter 12**
**Practicing Self-Care**

What does a well on a small farm have to do with replenishment strategies in ministry?

What are some of the reasons why pastoral ministry is so stressful? Which reason(s) listed in this chapter have challenged you?

How can pastors recover the "Sabbath Principle" in their ministries?